BONDING& BREAKING FREE

John Q. Baucom

D0124217

PYRANEE BOOKS

Zondervan Publishing House
Grand Rapids, Michigan

BONDING AND BREAKING FREE
Copyright © 1988 by John Q. Baucom

Pyranee Books are published by Zondervan Publishing House
1415 Lake Drive, S.E., Grand Rapids, Michigan 49506

Library of Congress Cataloging in Publication Data

Baucom, John Q.
  Bonding and breaking free.

  Bibliography: p.
  1. Child rearing. 2. Parent and child. I. Title.
HQ769.B3379 1988   649'.1   87-34515
ISBN 0-310-20521-2

Printed in the United States of America

88 89 90 91 92 / LP / 10 9 8 7 6 5 4 3 2 1

To my mother, Lois, and to the memory of my father, John Quincy Baucom. God gave me wonderful parents, and I am grateful.

Others have played parenting roles in my life, and I would like to acknowledge and thank them:

Carl Lee Morgan and Ethel Stogner Morgan
Rev. Barret Gilmer and Mary Dudley Gilmer
Rev. Jim Murray and Elaine Murray
Rev. Joe McLeod and Virginia McLeod
Jack Smith
Joe Swanner
Andor Toldy
Col. John Keplinger and Nellie Keplinger
Dr. Clinton Phillips

ACKNOWLEDGMENTS

Many people helped me with this book, and it's impossible to thank them all. I would, however, like to mention several.

Bennie, my wife, helped with the entire manuscript and had responsibility for most of the research. Maxie Zieglar's typing and editorial input was invaluable.

Others who deserve thanks include Winford Hendrix, John Talbird, Nancy Wright, and the late Dr. Clint Phillips.

I would like to add a special thanks to the many people I have met and worked with in counseling, seminars, and workshops whose stories appear in this book. I've changed names and circumstances to protect their identities, but their emotional strength and concern for others is genuine.

CONTENTS

INTRODUCTION

April 4, 1982

I sat across from the young CPA. Although he was quite a few years younger than I, he had legitimately earned several million dollars during his lifetime.

"That's incredible," I exclaimed. "How do you do it? I want some of that Midas touch. I'm tired of just barely scraping by."

"Well," he drawled, leaning over, "it's real simple. I sit in an office all day long and listen to what my clients do wrong. Then I go out and do the opposite with my money. Basically, I learn from everybody else's mistakes."

"Great," I smiled. "Guess I should have taken accounting."

The accountant's face grew grim. "No, John," he shook his head. "Wait a minute. I'm the one who has the problems. I'm the one who's here for therapy. Sure, I've got money. But you've got happiness. I've been married four times. All my kids hate me. I have an ulcer. Money can't cure all that. If it could, it would have already.

"The way I figure it," he continued, "is that you do the same thing I do, except you do it with people's emotional mistakes. You hear how they mess up their lives—their marriages, their kids, their happiness—and then you do the opposite. You've got it made. You ought to write a book about it."

November 11, 1987

Dr. Margaret Mead, a world renowned anthropologist, spent her life studying human beings and our relationships to one another, our culture, and our environment. It was Dr. Mead, I understand, who said, "With the appearance of the two-bathroom home, Americans forgot how to cooperate." I agree, and I would go two steps further. I believe that with the arrival of the two-car family we forgot how to associate, and with the coming of the two-television home we forgot how to communicate.

In our society, the family has assumed a subordinate position to industry, progress, and technology. Family is no longer the central unit of society. And children are paying the exhorbitant price: two million attempt suicide per year; ninety-two percent experiment with drugs before reaching age 18; more than 50,000 run away from home per year; forty percent of those are "thrown away" by their parents; and more than 1.2 million become victims of abuse.

My good friend and former pastor, Dr. Winford Hendrix, once said, "Let's learn from each other's mistakes, because I don't have time to make them all myself." In his own peculiar way, he showed sensitive but biting wisdom. While writing this book, I have followed his counsel, as well as that of the CPA I spoke to years ago.

Parenting, in my opinion, is our most important responsibility. My prayer is that each of you may learn from the research, the affirmations, and the mistakes presented in this book. If questions arise that the book does not answer, I invite your inquiries at the address below. May God bless each of you, and may Christ's love flourish among us all.

Dr. John Baucom
7433 Preston Circle
Chattanooga, TN 37421

GOOD IDEA!

Two are better than one, because they have a
good return for their work: If one falls down, his
friend can help him up. But pity the man who falls
and has no one to help him up! Also, if two lie
down together, they will keep warm. But how can
one keep warm alone? Though one may be
overpowered, two can defend themselves. A cord
of three strands is not quickly broken.

—Ecclesiastes 4:9–12

The deepest need of man, then, is the need to
overcome his separateness, to leave the prison of
his aloneness. The absolute failure to achieve this
aim means insanity, because the pain of complete
isolation can be overcome only by such a radical
withdrawal from the world outside that the feeling
of separation disappears—because the world
outside, from which one is separated, has disap-
peared.

—Erich Fromm

1

Love and Accept Your Child

LABOR HAD LASTED over thirty hours and many unexpected problems occurred. Things had gone wrong. There was so much I didn't understand. Attempts at interpreting masked faces proved futile.

My soul cried for this to be over. My wife, Bennie, alternated between unconsciousness and a delirious haze. I was scared, tired, sleepy, and felt very alone. It was as if aliens from outer space had invaded my life. Machines made noises I didn't understand, and physicians arrived I hadn't met. "Specialists," I was told.

But nobody said why.

I was an "older" first-time father, and my wife was an "older" first-time mother. The prenatal care she had received was the finest obstetrics could offer. There were continuous, but unsolicited, assurances that everything would be just fine.

Somehow these unsought bits of advice had the reverse of their intended effect. Why, I wondered, do they tell me

*everything is going to be fine? In my mind that could only
mean something was wrong. I had wanted a son all my adult
life. I would name him after my father, I thought. It would be
an appropriate memorial to a man who died before my tenth
birthday.*

*I became quite anxious toward the completion of the
pregnancy. For some reason I was scared things might not be
right. Nightmares haunted my sleep. But this wasn't one of
those nightmares. The rhythmic beeping of a heart monitor
returned me to the delivery room.*

*"Dr. Baucom, why don't you leave and get some rest?" A
nurse asked.*

*"No, thanks. I'm okay." This was the fourth time I was
asked to leave. For the fourth time I refused. I wanted to cry
out loud but was too scared. I couldn't miss this. We had
waited eleven years for our first child to be born.*

*He was finally delivered by cesarean section. He was blue,
and the umbilical cord was wrapped where I knew it shouldn't
be. His head rose to a peak and seemed dented. He gasped. But
he was alive!*

At this point I began to understand love.

IMPERFECT LOVE

Several years ago, I asked seminar participants to recall a
relationship in which they had felt unconditionally accepted
and absolutely loved. After expanding on the quality of
unconditional acceptance, it came as no surprise that only a
few could recall even one relationship in which they felt truly
accepted—regardless of their behavior. Unfortunately, this
scenario has been repeated dozens of times over the years in
both counseling sessions and seminars.

Our love and acceptance as parents is going to be
imperfect. Our children and their responses are going to be
equally imperfect. Yet one of the most often repeated mistakes

in parenting is expecting perfection, either in ourselves or in our children.

If I expect perfection from my children, I am placing totally unrealistic hopes and stress on us all. Their response, both behaviorally and emotionally, will reflect that stress. Expecting perfection from myself is equally devastating and will eventually affect both me and my family adversely. Healthy love acknowledges human flaws and accepts people as they are.

Recognizing this value may be easy, but its application is difficult at best. People are pretty much the same. Parents love their children, but love is not enough unless it makes allowances for and accepts imperfection. The meaning of this is as difficult for us to understand as it was for Mrs. Smith, whom I met after speaking at a seminar.

She waited for over an hour, hovering on the edge of our group, never coming close enough to speak. She was a short woman whose brown hair was pulled behind her head in a large bun. Her face was rather plain, not graced by makeup. She gazed at the floor and smiled shyly when looking up. Her leathered hands gripped a large, worn Bible which she held tightly against her body.

The conference was attended by a large number of people. Many had questions to ask aloud. Others wished to ask questions privately. It was taking much longer than I anticipated. Most had left by the time she finally inched toward me. I guessed she was probably the mother of a teenager.

"Dr. Baucom, I'm Mrs. Smith. Thank you for your program. It was very good." She offered her hand and I shook it.

"Thank you." I responded. "That's very kind. I'm glad you came. It was a good crowd."

"Well, we needed to hear you." She stopped and looked at the floor. Her head lowered as she cleared her throat. After a few seconds, she raised her eyes. "Can I talk to you for about ten minutes? I know your family is waiting, but I won't take long and it's very important."

"Sure. Ten minutes? Easy." I focused my eyes on her as she began to speak.

"I have a seventeen-year-old son. I've had to raise him by myself. My husband left fifteen years ago."

I could have predicted the rest of the story. Her son had been arrested several times. Currently, he was in a juvenile rehabilitation center. Mrs. Smith was struggling with guilt and self-criticism. She felt her son's predicament was her fault and wondered what she had done wrong.

"I don't want to do the same thing to his brother." By now she was crying aloud, no longer hiding her tears. I allowed her to continue. After a moment, she regained control.

"You believe in God." I commented as a fact, more than a question. My pause indicated to her I was awaiting a response.

"Yes." She seemed startled. "Yes, I do."

"Then do you believe God is perfect?" By now she was studying me with a curious frown on her brow. She shifted her worn Bible from one hand to the other.

"Well, yes. God is perfect." She nodded her head several times. The tears quickly dried from her eyes.

"Well, if God is perfect, then wouldn't he be a perfect parent?" I wondered aloud.

"Yes." She nodded again. "Yes. He certainly would be."

"And according to the Bible what happened to his children? Whatever became of Adam and Eve? How did they behave?"

She hesitated for a moment and then began to speak. "I see where you're going, but—"

"No," I interrupted her gently. "Wait. Now if anybody ever had a chance to be good kids, it was Adam and Eve, right? They had one-on-one contact with God. Their relationship was intense, intimate. If anybody could raise obedient children, wouldn't it be God?"

She hesitated again as if weighing the evidence. "Well, yes. Yes, I guess so." She looked at me with a hint of a smile.

"Okay," I continued. "So if God is perfect and he raises

imperfect children, how can you, who are imperfect, raise perfect children? You could do every conceivable thing right, and your kids would still end up imperfect. At some point they make their own choices just like Adam and Eve did. They might make unfortunate choices. There's no way you can be a perfect parent. I just don't think your guilt is going to help you or your children."

"So what do I do, give up?" She asked with a smile.

"No. I don't think so." I responded. "Give up your guilt, yes. Give up on your kids, no. I'd encourage you to accept them as being just like you—imperfect and unique. Love them regardless of what happens. Give them time and attention and recognize your limits. They are separate individuals and will make their own choices. Approach them as individuals and accept them that way."

We paused and stared at each other for a moment. She thanked me and left with my address. Since then we have exchanged letters on several occasions. She reports that both she and her children are happier and healthier. She let go of the stress of perfectionism.

UNCONDITIONAL ACCEPTANCE

Several years ago while conducting a seminar, I asked the participants to think of a specific relationship in which they felt loved. We then began listing the identifiable actions that resulted in the more abstract feeling of being loved. After struggling for over an hour, we collectively agreed that adequately defining love is nearly impossible, but all agreed that unconditional acceptance is a fundamental characteristic of love.

LEARNING FROM THE PAST

History presents us with several examples of children raised in an environment absent of love. The earliest record goes back to the thirteenth century. Emperor Frederick II (Frederick the Great) was apparently curious to see what language children would learn if they never heard anyone speak. He wondered if it would be the language of their biological parents or some other language such as Greek or Latin. So he began an experiment with a group of orphans. He instructed the foster mothers to feed and clothe the infants, but never to speak or interact with them in any way. By doing this, he thought the infants would learn the "natural" language. The emperor never discovered the answer to his question. Each baby died before speaking at all. They were fed and clothed and had their biological needs filled, but each individual child quickly died. Some have suggested that the lack of loving interaction with adults may have been one of the causes of early death.

Another illustration is found in the story of Victor, a child found in a French forest near Aveyron in the late eighteenth century. Although documented history is sketchy, Victor reportedly lived with wolves most of his early life. He ate berries and plants, walked on all fours, and often barked and howled. Victor lived as an untamed animal and, in fact, was referred to as the wild boy of Aveyron. When discovered by a monk, he was reportedly dangerous to other humans. Eventually the monks moved him into a monastery school and began trying to help him. Unfortunately, Victor died early in his "civilized life" before significant progress could be made. Apparently, the early void of human love and acceptance was the primary factor in his death.

A recent and more well-documented case illustrating the damage done by an absence of love and acceptance is found in the cases of Anna and Isabelle. Anna was discovered at the approximate age of six in 1938. Reportedly, she was being raised by her grandfather who kept her hidden in a closetlike space in the attic. She was fed and had her basic biological needs met but received only a minimal degree of interaction. When found, Anna was thought to be deaf and possibly even blind. She was unable to walk, talk, or feed herself. Anna was taken away from her grandfather and placed in a more nurturing home. She eventually learned to walk and achieved the maturity level of age two or three. However, the lack of early love had a cancerous effect. She died at age eleven.

Isabelle was discovered at approximately the same time as Anna and at nearly the same age. She also was kept isolated from the outside world in a dark room, watched over by her grandfather. However, unlike Anna, Isabelle was locked up with her mother, who was both deaf and mute. Apparently, the grandfather was embarrassed at the illegitimate birth of his granddaughter. When discovered, Isabelle also appeared deaf and mute, and her behavior around anyone other than her mother was described as animal-like.

Isabelle did have the advantage of her mother's love and, later, a team of very caring doctors to help her. As a result, by age eight, she reached an almost average level of intellectual and social development. She attended school with others. By age fourteen she finished sixth grade. Before long, it was impossible to distinguish Isabelle from her classmates. The difference in these two cases appears to be the significant impact of the love and acceptance Isabelle received from her mother. She was also helped by the team of doctors who cared for her after her discovery. Isabelle eventually was able to live a normal life.

UNDERSTANDING THE PRESENT

After hearing of these historical illustrations, one might wonder if children still sometimes suffer from lack of love and acceptance. The answer is yes. Although official statistics are difficult to come by, professionals in the medical and helping professions see people daily who suffer from the same malady. The problems can be found in toddlers, senior citizens, and all age ranges in between. Lack of love and acceptance can lead to lack of motivation. This can result in lack of meaning, lack of hope, and ultimately the lack of will to continue life.

By accepting your children unconditionally, you affirm them as being okay simply as they are. Unconditional acceptance is making the love you have free of ifs and buts, and basing it on the person rather than his or her performance. Unconditional acceptance is saying "I love you" rather than "I love you when you make good grades or when you're good."

Fred Rogers of "Mister Rogers Neighborhood" sends a daily dose of unconditional acceptance to his viewers. "You're special, and I love you just the way you are," he tells them. Similar to the apostle Paul's description of love, this approach does indeed "endure all things." It communicates to the child that she doesn't have to be perfect or different to earn love. The love and acceptance are given freely, in spite of messes, bad grades, or temper tantrums.

"We just can't take her home like this. You don't understand. I can't handle her fits anymore." Mrs. Webb leaned toward me in her chair. Her frosted hair was teased into a huge "beehive." She nervously clasped and unclasped her hands. Long, garish earrings dangled beneath her ears. She gestured wildly like a symphony conductor, orchestrating those of us in the office.

"Nobody wants you to put up with her fits, Mrs. Webb," I slowly began to explain. "But this isn't like going to a dentist and getting a tooth pulled. It's going to take time. And by responding this way to Cindy, you're doing precisely what she wants. There is no magic. I can't do a 'fit-ectomy.'"

Cindy and her father laughed at my explanation. The laughter was unnoticed by Mrs. Webb. "Well, just what am I supposed to do in the meantime?" she demanded. "She even makes me have fits. Is there anywhere we can put her?" Mrs. Webb had exhausted her psychological resources for dealing with Cindy's explosive outbursts. After visiting with several other family members, I began to have a clearer understanding of both Cindy and her mother.

I discovered that in reality, the entire family was volatile. There was constant, loud arguing, and occasional physical abuse. The parents often would drink until intoxicated and begin loud arguments that continued all night. During a later individual session, Cindy confessed she was intimidated by her mother and had never felt loved and accepted. She reported a long history of self-doubt dating back to preschool days.

At various times Cindy had suffered asthma, panic attacks, and phobias. She recalled getting nauseous in kindergarten and first grade to avoid going to school. She became sexually active at age fourteen and currently had plans of getting married before her eighteenth birthday. She explained about her boyfriend, "He just loves me, and makes me feel good, and can give me a baby who will love me no matter what." On interviewing other family members (including grandparents), I discovered Cindy had been an unwanted baby. Her current father was not her biological father. At birth, Cindy was rejected by her mother and at one time was diagnosed as suffering from "failure to thrive." The pediatrician suggested this was from lack of parental attention, although this is not the only possible cause.

What at first appeared to be the temper tantrum problem of an immature seventeen-year-old girl was in reality a family problem. Lack of love and acceptance during early childhood was the apparent origin. The effects permeated her entire life. Instead of hospitalization, Cindy needed the type of stability and security produced by a loving environment. Love and acceptance are necessary for healthy development. They provide children the safety from which to experiment and take chances, which are natural in emotionally healthy children. With each consecutive risk the child is reassured by the love and acceptance that only a parent can provide. This strengthens the child's confidence and makes her more likely to risk and grow again.

These risks are negotiated consecutively. If a child is not reassured at each level, then emotional, intellectual, and even physical development might stop at that point. In Cindy's case, she possessed the physical development of a seventeen-year-old, the intellectual development of a fourteen-year-old, but the emotional maturity of a mere eight-year-old. It was apparently unsafe for her to risk a great deal beyond that point. And without such risk, mature emotional development was impossible. So Cindy, like thousands of her peers, looked elsewhere. In her case, she thought the answer could be found through a sexual relationship with her boyfriend. Well-publicized reports indicate many thousands of others attempt running away from their problems through physical escape and sometimes even suicide.

Dr. Seymour Perlin, Director of the National Youth Suicide Prevention Center, estimates two million teenagers will attempt suicide in the coming year. The American Medical Association estimates one out of nine teenagers will be addicted to alcohol or some other drug before the age of fifteen. That doesn't even include those who will become addicted after age fifteen. We all are aware of the frequency of teenage prostitution, sexual promiscuity, and the high incidence of theft and burglaries by juveniles. In my opinion, all of these examples reflect the unfulfilled search for unconditional acceptance and love that could be provided by parents.

This assertion is well-supported by scientific research. One study found that parents with accepting attitudes produced children who were not only more secure but who had higher self-esteem as well. A second study found that accepting attitudes even produced benign physiological responses.

A galvanic response (GSR) device measures perspiration on the palm as an indication of nervousness. The device is a small electronic instrument with a sensor attached around the finger tip of the person being questioned. One researcher measured anxiety as it was affected by an interviewer's acceptance of the interviewee. At any point, if the interviewer's attitude grew less accepting, the amount of GSR significantly increased. This implied that when a person does not feel accepted they become anxious. Their level of nervous sweat increases! We could probably all agree that we feel emotionally better when accepted. But this research indicates that we even feel better neurologically and physiologically when accepted unconditionally.

PRACTICING THE TRUTH

The qualities of love and unconditional acceptance (although admittedly imperfect) have been discussed throughout literature of the ages. They have been found to be the basis of good parenting in research studies as well as practice. But we are not born with these tools. They must be learned. We are not born with the innate ability to love and unconditionally accept others. Nor are we somehow born with the magic ability to be good parents. Parenting is not scientific. Due to the unpredictability of human choice, which any parent can testify that even day-old infants have, we can't assume anything *always* works. As humans, we must consider each child unique. And even though it's not a science, parenting is an art form that can be improved by keeping each unique child in mind. As far as is humanly possible, we want to avoid using trial-and-error learning on children..

The capacity to love and accept your children unconditionally needs to be nurtured and practiced. Reading about the concepts is a beginning. It will probably take additional reading, thought, and study to begin truly understanding the qualities being discussed. By following the reading with practice, you will perhaps begin to master each concept.

Practice can take many forms. Attendance at parenting seminars is one place to get some practical training. Discussing these issues with professionals or other parents is another place. If you currently have no children, babysitting is a good way to practice parenting skills.

Before Bennie and I had children, we raised two Dobermans, three cats, a couple of snakes, relatives, and several neighbors! Then, later in life we started on our own family. Since that time I have recommended to dozens of childless couples that they practice their parenting skills by raising pets together. Some very enlightening lessons can be learned by doing so.

Steve and Carla visited me during their third year of marriage to discuss some problems they were experiencing. During the session, Carla revealed they wanted to have children in the next two years. At my suggestion, they purchased a Doberman pup and began taking him through obedience training. Up to this point, the young couple had very little responsibility for anyone other than themselves. Suddenly, there was the added burden of a third party—the dog. There was a feeding schedule, paper (potty) training, daily walks, watering, obedience school, and practice (homework). The pup also demanded emergency visits to the vet, needed ear clipping and baths, caused negotiations with the neighbors over boxwoods that had been dug up, howled at 2:00 A.M. during the full moon, and had to have a dog sitter when they traveled out of town.

The couple discovered they had different values. Steve was very protective of the Doberman, but Carla grew weary of "puppy-parenting." Steve expected the pup to sleep in their bed. Carla said, "No way, one of us is going outside." He later became upset with Carla's strict approach to discipline when muddy dog prints covered the carpet. Carla wanted to spank the pup. Steve disagreed, and a long argument ensued. This resulted in a 1:00 A.M. phone call to me. We met three days later. It was my first time for a Doberman to be included in family therapy! It was also a valuable lesson for Steve and Carla. They waited five more years to have children. During the interim they were able to reconcile the personality differences that caused their disagreement. They made their mistakes on a dog rather than on children.

Incidently, I also make the same recommendation to parents of teenagers. Give the teenager responsibility for raising several pets. This can be an excellent way to learn parenting principles and to begin appreciating the responsibility of "child-rearing." Practicing your parenting skills on a couple of one-hundred-pound Dobermans can be a valuable learning experience for people of any age!

Good parenting skills must be practiced time and time again to become good habits. None of these qualities occur naturally. Learning to love and unconditionally accept your children is a process to begin now and continue for life. Still, it is a process that will never reach perfection.

I was allowed to hold my son before he was taken away to the neonatal intensive care unit. He was alive, and would "probably be okay," I was told. His mother was being rushed in the opposite direction, also to intensive care. I started to run in one direction and then reversed to head in the other.

"Who do I go with?" I finally asked aloud to no one in particular.

"Check on your son. Bennie will be okay. So will he, I promise." It was our family physician. He was the only person I recognized. "Go on, John. Go see about him. I'll take care of Bennie."

She was still somewhat delirious. I reached down and whispered, "He's got a dimple in his chin. The dimple you wanted. He's going to be okay."

She smiled and squeezed my hand.

As they took her away I rushed to find neonatal intensive care. I got lost in the maze of the hospital and accidentally found my mother who had arrived from out of town. We hugged each other. I didn't know she was coming and never felt more grateful to see her. Finally, I could relax.

She let me settle down before saying a word.

"Dr. Haren says they'll be okay," she reassured me.

"I know. I believe him. I'm just tired. I've never felt like this before. I want that little boy to live so badly, I would give up anything. He can have my eyes, my heart, my brain, my life, anything he needs. I would give it up without hesitation, without question. I've never felt like this before. I mean, I love

Bennie, but this is so different." I paused as my eyes began to fill with tears.

"I know, Son," my mother responded. "I know. I'm glad you understand. Now maybe you know how I feel about you. But more importantly, now maybe you know how much God loved us. He gave up his Son and watched him die for us. That's real love."

I paused and as my eyes cleared, I understood. "I understand that now, Mom." And for once in my life, I finally comprehended my mother's strength. Later, I checked on my new son and my wife. I gave thanks for all of our lives. Then I rested.

There was a sense of peace. I finally understood unconditional acceptance. It is the ultimate expression of love.

IMPROVING YOUR PARENTING ART

1. What is your first memory of love being shown toward you?

2. What other incidents from the past helped form your concept of love?

3. In your own life, who have been true Christlike models of love toward you? What characteristics of this person or these persons have influenced you most?

4. How have you specifically shown love or lack of love toward your children?

5. Think of a time when you were accepted unconditionally. What did it feel like? Is there anyone that you accept in a similar way? Is there anyone who accepts you now unconditionally?

PARENTING EXERCISES

Find children at different ages and interview them concerning their understanding of love. As an example, speak to children of the following ages: 5, 7, 9, 11, 13, 15, and 17. How do their descriptions differ? What do you notice about the complexity and clarity of their definition? With younger children, ask such questions as follow: What is love? How do you show love? Who shows you love? With teenagers, ask them to describe their ideas about love, the actions demonstrated by love, and who they know who really loves other people.

Live a life of love, just as Christ loved us and gave himself up for us as a fragrant offering and sacrifice to God. . . . Be very careful, then, how you live—not as unwise but as wise, making the most of every opportunity, because the days are evil. . . . No one ever hated his own body, but he feeds and cares for it, just as Christ does the church.

—*Ephesians 5:2, 15, 16, 29*

Teaching is leaving a vestige of oneself in the development of another, and surely the child is a bank where you can deposit your most precious treasures.

—*Eugene P. Bertin*

2

Spend Time With Your Child

ONE PARTICULAR evening I had received several stressful calls at the beginning of a radio program. One caller was depressed. Someone else had experienced the death of a parent. A woman had recently gone through a divorce and was hurting. I had time for one short call before the break and decided to go ahead and take it. The voice was of an adult male.

"Explain something to me, John," he began. "I really don't understand. You work with a lot of teenagers and families; maybe you can figure it out for me.

"I want to know what's going on with today's teenagers. Why do we have all these problems with them today? You've got drugs, pregnancies, and suicide.

"I've got two teenage girls myself. Their friends are flipping out all over the place. I grew up during the sixties in the drug scene. That was a crazy time. But this is much worse. What in the world's going on today?"

Everything seemed to stand still for a moment. Quite honestly, I wanted to sigh and throw my hands up in bewilderment, but that's not something you can take the time to do on live, call-in radio. After only a breath, I responded.

IMPORTANCE OF TIME

Years ago I heard a story about Pablo Picasso, the great artist. Apparently, at the time, he was eating in a French restaurant. An admirer approached with a napkin and asked him to draw something on it. "Anything," she said. "I'll pay you whatever your fee is. Just draw something."

As the story goes, Picasso took the napkin and sketched for five minutes. He returned it to the admirer and said his fee would be forty thousand dollars.

Suddenly, admiration turned to disbelief.

"Maestro," she demanded. "It's beautiful, but how can you charge such money when it only took you five minutes?"

"No, you're wrong," Picasso responded. "It's taken me my entire life."

Picasso took many years to develop his skill as an artist. What appeared to be spontaneous scribbling to an admirer, was actually the result of more than fifty years spent in training, practicing, and studying his art.

In much the same way, spending meaningful time with children produces beautiful lives. Picasso was able to do what he did because he had invested time in perfecting his art. As parents we need to do the same.

Benjamin Franklin suggested: "Do not squander time, for that is the stuff life is made of." Franklin was correct. The issue is made more complex because as a parent there are pressure-filled demands placed on every second. Time is the primary commodity we have to offer. And if you are an average American you are spending too little of that commodity with your children. Yet more than anything else, time is what they need.

In counseling, conferences, and seminars I constantly hear the same complaint. There is not enough time to go around. Repeatedly, lack of time is rated as the biggest stress on family life. It's the most frequent complaint from children, wives, and husbands. One father, a physician, told of being confronted by his minister over his sporadic church attendance on Sunday nights.

"You tell me who I am going to hurt then, pastor," he began. "Should I hurt my children by not spending time with them; my wife by not spending time with her; my hospitalized patients by not giving them attention; or my body by not giving it any exercise; or perhaps my mind by not giving it any rest. You tell me who to sacrifice in order to attend three or four weekly church services and I'll do it. But you be responsible, not me, because I don't want to have to make that decision. I simply don't have enough time."

The most important thing you can do for your children is to provide them with meaningful time. An important part of that is getting to know their friends in a sincere and caring way. This is usually not as difficult as parents think it will be. Odds are, no other adult, other than their own parents, is spending time getting to know them at all. And time with caring adults is something adolescents crave but get little of in our culture today. If you gain their trust, your child's friends will begin coming to you if your own child gets into some emotional trouble. They become a psychological "early warning signal" and will usually notify you of impending danger. As an adult, expanding your care and time to include your child's friends is mutually beneficial to all parties. Everybody wins.

Spending meaningful time with your children is vital, both for their health and yours. Over the past several years, debate has raged concerning quantity and quality time. One extreme argues that quality is of no significance and that quantity is what matters. The other extreme argues that quantity is irrelevant and that quality is what matters. Both concepts warrant further inquiry.

PARENTS AND TIME

Starting at least as far back as 1945, child care experts have associated child-rearing with mothering. Mothering once was considered a full-time job, exclusive of input from fathers. Early writers in the field of child development referred to a mothering instinct as being natural in all women. Some even suggested a woman could be a good parent just by virtue of being a woman. There are indeed some ways in which mothers are better suited for child-rearing. As an example, they have breasts and produce milk to nourish a child. In fact, an infant's cry can trigger the flow of the hormone oxytocin, which causes nipple erection and enables the child to nurse.

Yet to say all women can "instinctively" mother or parent a child is unfair. Mothering and all good parenting skills, including fathering, are learned. And indeed there may be cases when someone other than the mother of a child could serve as a more competent primary caretaker.

Much has been said over the past few years about the effects of working mothers, and most of it has aroused tremendous emotional response. Without doubt, children need intense care. However, research seems to indicate that after the first few years of life, the quality of care is more important than whether or not the care comes from a full-time mother.

Perhaps, for a change, someone should focus on the effects of working fathers. Children need to spend time with both parents. As an example, some research indicates that if extended absence of the father occurs before a male child reaches age four, he is apt to be less masculine, more dependent on peers, less assertive, and less involved in athletics. Occasional absence of the father after age four, however, has little effect on boys' sex role development.

The myth that child-rearing is exclusively a woman's job has proven to be exceptionally dangerous to children. In no way is it supported by research, and fathers who avoid their responsibility are far more numerous than mothers who do the same. The responsibility of spending meaningful time with children belongs to both parents.

There is little evidence to indicate that a mother working outside the home will inherently harm a child after the first few years. In fact, the opposite may be true. This has been supported by studies going as far back as the 1930s. The evidence has consistently agreed. Cross-cultural research has also supported these findings. In general, employed mothers do not cheat their children. Surprisingly, they often spend as much time interacting with their children as full-time mothers. Employed mothers also appear to rate themselves more satisfied than do full-time mothers. As a result, they seem to enjoy parenting more.

Society has changed greatly over the past twenty-five years, and these changes have caused parenting roles to change as well. The family unit is no longer what we once fantasized it would be. The Ozzie and Harriet family of the 1950s no longer exists, if it ever did in any form other than television fiction. Our child-rearing practices actually reflect the demands society places on the family because it adapts to these demands. Other societies function in a similar manner.

Some of these societies have experimented with alternative ways of spending meaningful time with their children. The Nayars of India, several American Indian groups, and the more researched kibbutz of Israel have provided valuable information on child-rearing. The kibbutz is, in most ways, an agricultural community. The members share a collective lifestyle and most property is communally owned. In the kibbutz, children are cared for primarily by nursery staff members. Parents visit children regularly and meet their primary emotional needs.

Discipline and instruction, however, are the responsibilities of the professional nursery staff. Recently, in the kibbutz, parents have been taking a more active role with their children. Yet their role still involves more nurture than discipline.

Many kibbutz-reared children are adults today with children of their own. Generally speaking, these communally reared children have much lower rates of emotional disturbance or family problems than traditionally reared children. Otherwise, systematic observation, testing, and clinical assessment have shown that kibbutz children are average-to-above-average both intellectually and physically.

Although no research is totally conclusive, it appears that communally reared children are healthy and successful by all standards of measurement. The implication seems to be that the quality of time parents spend with children is an extremely important consideration. It may be that quality time is the most important parenting issue, and one on which we have not focused enough attention.

QUANTITY TIME

Some people view quality and quantity as opposite ends of a spectrum. They are not, however, mutually exclusive. In reality, quality time is important, but so is quantity. My experience has convinced me that before you can have any quality time, you must first invest quantity time. Any relationship takes time to establish. Weeks are needed to build anything as complex as a human friendship. But the hours must be packed with quality discussion and learning. The concepts are complementary in that respect.

As an example, people can spend thirty years of quantity time together working side by side in a noisy factory and develop only a superficial relationship. On the other hand, I have grown extremely close to people through intense private discussion during a six-hour plane ride. It takes both quality and quantity to build a relationship. Billy's story reflects this idea.

Billy was in the hospital as a result of injuries incurred in a suicide attempt. A week before his seventeenth birthday he had blown off his lower jaw with a .357 magnum. He had attempted to blow his entire life away but had failed. The disfiguring injury left him even more depressed than before. A lengthy hospitalization followed. Intensive care for a month included several operations to save his life and to begin rebuilding his jaw. The rebuilding was not totally successful, but Billy's emotional condition was deteriorating so rapidly that it became his physician's major concern. He referred Billy for counseling. Billy really didn't care. He didn't want to live anymore.

I began spending time with Billy by merely sitting in his room with him. Some days when he said nothing, I said nothing. If he looked at me, I returned his look. If he looked at the floor, so did I. At the close of these sessions, I assured Billy that I would return the next day and told him that he could call me if he wanted to talk before then. This continued for over two weeks, thirty minutes a day.

Billy's withdrawal was not only from me. He withdrew from life itself. At one point he refused to eat for several days. During this time, he did not once appear to recognize me or even seem to know I was there. His depression was extremely severe and dangerous. Several physicians monitored Billy medically and administered needed medication. Billy stubbornly refused to improve, and I stubbornly refused to quit visiting him.

Three weeks after my first visit, I finally got a response from him, albeit a nonverbal one. Three days later he spoke to me. A week later we began walking together on the hospital grounds. At this point, the psychotherapeutic process began in earnest. But the foundation of that process had begun one month before. It had taken the preceding period of constant daily visits (quantity time) before any trust developed. During that month, the words spoken between us would not fill one-half a page of this book. Remarkably, one week later, the discussion was endless. This is when quality work began. A relationship of trust would never have happened without the amount of time spent the previous month. Some psychotherapists and writers say quantity time is all that's important. "Just spend time with your children," we're told. "The quality will take care of itself." I could not disagree more. One of the primary reasons for spending a quantity of time is for the reward of quality.

QUALITY TIME

Quality time demands high energy and intensity. It is a time of openness to the child, focusing upon his or her uniqueness. It is priority time spent on developing the relationship rather than on some other activity, such as commuting to school, eating supper, or watching TV. The way quality time is spent will vary with the child. It may be playing with an eight-month-old's rattle or wrestling with a toddler. It may be going out of your way so your four-year-old can see a cow or horse and stop to pet them. It may be helping your second grader with a tough assignment or listening when he tells you about his "dumb music lesson." It may be going for a long bike ride in the park or a boat ride during the summer.

Years later quality time may be a lengthy discussion about rock groups, hair styles, or whether to play linebacker or fullback. Maybe it's spent discussing dating habits or boyfriend problems. Or it might be spent preparing for a 10-kilometer run and later crossing the finish line together with hands clasped and held high. It can be a long ride in the country, locked in the car together for a couple of hours with the radio turned off. It could be a ski trip together during the winter.

Quality time can also be reading together, talking about things, or holding hands at any age. It can be walking in the woods, downtown, or on a neighborhood street. It can be discussing a lecture you heard or the president's public address. It can be talking about the quality of your relationship or how to make it better. However, it's not just limited to talking about problems. It's also not limited to mothers, although historically that has been the accepted cultural belief.

INTENSITY

Quality time can often be both brief and intense. It is these intense times that can be life-changing. When my eldest son, Keppy, was only two years old, we first shared the splendor of focused time together while snow skiing. I was delighted to discover that tiny boots and skis were made for children his age. I fitted him with a set and off we went. Skiing, though fun, is work for me. To him it seemed to be no work at all.

I spread my skis and inverted them into a snowplow. Placing Keppy and his skis between mine, I leaned over, grasped his shoulders, and we were off. By the end of the day we had skied most of the beginner and intermediate slopes. My back, thighs, and arms all throbbed. But the profound joy we shared during that experience far outweighed the pain. Our intensity was composed of several key factors: physical contact, shared experience, cold air, snow, the sound of our skis skimming over the snow, speed, wind against our skin, conversation, and high emotion. It was one of the most treasured experiences that he and I have ever shared. And although we've skied together several times since then, that first time was most memorable. I shared the same experience with my second son, Chip, shortly after his second birthday!

I recall reading about a study completed several years ago

involving winners of National Merit Scholarships. These high achieving students had won scholarships to major universities based on the merits of their academic performance. Researchers interviewed a large number of scholarship winners from the past twenty-five years. Each was asked which of their high-school teachers they remembered as having the greatest impact on their development. Without fail, it was the teacher who took an intense personal interest in the student's individual goals and welfare. The students overlooked the easiest, the most difficult, and the funniest teachers. It was always the one who expressed an interest in the scholar more as a *person* than a student. Ralph Waldo Emerson aptly expressed the reason for this phenomenon when he said, "The secret of education is respecting the pupil."

As parents, we could take a similar cue. Expressing interest in our children because they are human beings will be rewarded. We can accomplish this in a variety of ways. Conversations oriented to our children's interests and hobbies can help achieve this goal. Similarly, time spent on activities that our children enjoy can be a selfless way to express interest in them. This is especially true if the child knows it's something we don't particularly enjoy. Taking long walks or drives with our children individually can lead to intimate and honest conversations.

An accepting, uncritical focus on our children's interests, at any opportunity, will strengthen their self-esteem. The lack of meaningful time and intensity leaves its mark. But so does its presence. Concentrated attention can heal emotional wounds. It doesn't have to be elaborate. It doesn't even have to last very long. But it's the essence of life.

My father died when I was nine years old. Our relationship was too brief. But in nine intensity-packed years, he had a significant impact on my life. The memories I carry of him are torn and faded like old photographs with worn edges. Sometimes they're almost impossible to recognize. I wish I could restore them, but I can't. I have only a few memories, but they're etched permanently in my mind. One is so powerful it's as if it's happening this moment. I have chill bumps on my forearms as I write about it.

The memorable experience happened in the mid-1950s. My dad had a flattop haircut, as did nearly everyone else back then. We were riding in a 1955 Buick with the windows open. It was a beautiful spring afternoon as we drove through the countryside. The warm air rushed against my face as I stood in the back seat, my arms wrapped around his neck. He drove the car with his left hand and reached his right arm behind him and around my neck. My cheek rubbed up and down on the stubbly hair of his neck. He was wearing Old Spice after-shave. I can still smell it. I hear him say, "I love you, Son." And I return, "I love you too, Daddy."

The entire exchange probably took less than ten seconds. But it was very intense. The impact will last my entire life. Soon after that interaction my father died. If he were still alive, he probably wouldn't even recall the incident. It may have meant very little to him. But it was an eternal gift to a nine-year-old boy who mourned his father's death a year later.

Thank God for intensity. It is the most meaningful way to spend time with your children.

The caller's question left me a wide open window. I could close it by ignoring the issue or I could take a deep breath of the breeze coming through it and try to answer his question. The caller sounded sincere, so I took a deep breath and began.

"You said you do have teenagers of your own," I commented.

"Yes, I do," he assured me. "And I'm having a bunch of problems with them too."

"Well," I offered. "Perhaps I could be of more help to you if there are particular problems you'd like me to address."

"I know you can do that," he responded. "But really, I'm more interested in a general opinion. What do you think? I am seriously puzzled with all that's going on. My daughter's best

friend overdosed last night. We just found out this morning. Life seems so much more serious to these kids. I don't know if the stakes are that much higher or what. Even back when LSD was so popular, kids didn't kill themselves like they do today."

I paused for a moment, wondering how best to respond.

"Well," I pondered aloud. "I hear you asking for my opinion. There is no scientific answer, at least that I know. I'll give you my opinion, but that's all it is. It's probably no better than anyone else's. Is that okay?"

"Sure," he quietly replied. "That's all I wanted."

"First of all, I don't think this country has a teenage problem. It's more a family problem. And beyond that it's more a society problem. You see, for years, I think adult society has been trying to sell our youth this materialistic value system. And I think the kids finally bought it.

"They have it all—the cars, the stereos, the computers. But I think they're finally figuring out that they've been sold a bill of goods. Quite frankly, I think they have, on an unconscious level, rejected our offer and are collectively giving us a symbolic slap in the face. They have realized that all these things don't matter.

"Over the past fifty years, corporations have replaced the American family as the primary unit of society. We respond to what's best for industry, not what's best for the family. And I think teenagers have figured it out.

"I don't think they care about the cars, the stereos, or really the company you work for. They care about you. And that's what they want. Your time, your presence, your intensity. They want you to be there in flesh and blood.

"And most teenagers today aren't getting that. So that's what I think. Maybe I'm right; maybe I'm not. I don't mean to step on anybody's toes. That's just my opinion. It's not a teenage problem at all. It's a problem with our way of life."

There was silence.

"God bless you," he finally said. "I'll bet you're right."

IMPROVING YOUR PARENTING ART

1. Study the priorities in your life such as yourself, family, extended family, friends, and work. Decide what percentage of your time is spent in each area. After surveying the results, determine if you are satisfied. If not, reassign a written percentage of time to those areas you wish to change.

2. Study your own style of interacting with others. Where is your primary focus of attention during these interactions— on them or on yourself?

3. If you knew your child had only six months to live, how would you spend your time with him?

4. Listen to what your child says. What can you learn about her needs from her words?

5. When your children are grown, how do you think they will characterize the time you spent with them as children?

PARENTING EXERCISES

1. Determine to spend a realistic amount of time per week (from five minutes to five hours) with each child, separately. No other family members or friends should be involved in this special time.

2. Within limits, allow the child to choose how you will spend the time.

3. During your time together, focus intensely on your child's needs, thoughts, and feelings. Avoid focusing on your own thoughts, problems, or schedules.

4. Suggest the following activities: play, talk, swing, read, help with school work, go to a park, a beach, a forest, attend church, spend time with the child's friends.

5. Keep all appointments with your child. Then, after thirty days, evaluate the results by discussing them with each child privately. Decide if you will continue the plan as it is or revise it to better meet both your needs.

GOOD THINKING!

You see, really and truly, apart from the things you
can pick up (the dressing and the proper way of
speaking, and so on), the difference between a
lady and a flower girl is not how she behaves but
how she's treated. I shall always be a flower girl to
Professor Higgins because he always treats me as
a flower girl and always will; but I know I can be
a lady to you because you always treat me as a
lady and always will.

—*George B. Shaw*, Pygmalion

Therefore, as we have opportunity, let us do good
to all people.

—*Galatians 6:10*

3

Set Your Child Up
to Win

AT A MORNING seminar I was discussing the importance of
attitude in working with teenagers. I spoke of "labels," belief
systems, and basic life positions. Apparently, during my
commentary I aroused an emotional response within one of
the participants. I noted her reaction as she made attempts to
fight away tears and later dried her eyes. I wasn't aware what
she was responding to, but I was curious.

During lunch I decided to seek her out and ask if she
would be willing to discuss her response. I located her as she
was also looking for me. Not only was she willing to share her
responses, but she had intended to discuss it later. Her story
was unique and also universal as it revealed emotional pain
experienced from negative labeling and expectations.

"I cried," she said, "because you were talking about me."

PYGMALION EFFECT

In the mid-1960s Dr. Robert Rosenthal began investigating the ways one person's expectations can influence the behavior of another. In one early experiment he randomly divided laboratory rats into two groups. He falsely designated one group as fast learners and the second group slow learners. In reality, the rats all learned at the same pace.

Dr. Rosenthal convinced his students the designations were accurate and then directed them to perform certain tests. "You will probably find the low-scoring rats doing the worst," he added. When they returned with results, Dr. Rosenthal was intrigued. The students said the rats labeled as "fast learners" scored higher, and the rats labeled as "slow learners" scored lower. Yet, the students claimed to be objective and fair in their testing! These and similar results puzzled Dr. Rosenthal, and it took years of advanced research to shed more light on his discovery.

Robert Rosenthal was not the first person to have an interest in the power of expectations. In Greek mythology, a Cypriot sculptor named Pygmalion fell in love with a statue that he was creating. He named the statue Galatea and viewed her as the perfect woman. As the myth goes, Pygmalion's love was so strong and his belief in Galatea so great that Aphrodite eventually brought the statue to life. Naturally, they lived happily ever after, so it must be a myth. Years later, author George Bernard Shaw brought the same theme to attention again. His play entitled *Pygmalion* later became the famed musical *My Fair Lady*. In the play, a distinguished, but conceited linguist, Professor Henry Higgins, is walking with his friend Colonel Pickering when they come upon the urchin flower girl Liza Doolittle. In her cockney accent, she attempts to sell them flowers. Professor Higgins acts offended at her desecration of the king's English and becomes very critical.

Then, on a bet from Colonel Pickering, Higgins suggests that by changing the way Liza speaks he could change her personality. In fact, he boasts, she could be passed off as a duchess at a royal reception. Colonel Pickering accepts his bet and the test begins.

He spends hours, days, and weeks drilling her. Teaching Liza to speak properly becomes more of a challenge than Professor Higgins anticipated. Even though highly frustrated at times, he never gives up. More importantly his confidence and belief in himself doesn't falter—at least in front of Liza. Professor Higgins's belief in himself, his ability to teach, and the propriety of the king's English are supreme. His belief in Liza is less! However, his self-confidence is more powerful than his doubt in Liza. And the confidence of his belief is so contagious it eventually infects her too.

"She's got it! By Jove, I think she's got it," he finally exclaims in *My Fair Lady*. Within the allotted time period, she does indeed have it. Liza has perfected her speech. Several nights later she successfully poses as a duchess at a royal reception. No one ever suspects she had been a flower girl. Professor Higgins wins the bet. But Colonel Pickering wins her heart. Even though Professor Higgins's belief in himself is great, he still thinks of Liza as a flower girl. Colonel Pickering, on the other hand, views her as a lady. Indeed, in Colonel Pickering's eyes Liza is even a duchess.

"I can be a lady to you," Liza suggests, "because you always treat me as a lady and always will."

Liza implies here that expectations are far more important than reality! In essence, Liza has defined the Pygmalion effect. A person's expectations can influence the outcome of an event far more powerfully than the reality of the event itself. If you expect your child to be a duchess, she's likely to perform as one. If you expect her to be a loser or troublemaker, on the other hand, she'll probably perform to those expectations. It's pretty simple. Positive treatment is more likely to cause positive outcome. Negative treatment is more likely to cause negative outcome.

A belief or attitude can influence more than just other

people. It can also influence actual events. This is proven regularly, sometimes with very dramatic results. As a hypothetical example, on Monday I hear a rumor that my bank is going to close. Fearing I'll lose my money, I decide to be at the bank early Tuesday morning to withdraw my money. But before that I call my sister and best friend to ask them if they have heard the rumor. They not only decide to take out their money, but they also call several of their friends. And the pattern continues.

As a result, early the next morning several dozen people are lined up outside the bank. Inquiring drivers pass as the line grows ever longer. Soon, a radio news team appears on the scene. Before long a television crew approaches. Several curious police officers accompany them.

"Haven't you heard?" someone echoes. "The bank's going to collapse. Today is the last day to pull your money out. If it's not out by midnight, you'll never get it."

This comment is broadcast citywide and soon picked up by the national networks. The line at the bank extends to the corner and down the side street. Tempers flare as people begin shoving to get closer. A few minutes later, the unsuspecting bank employees arrive. They haven't heard of the problem, but they decide this many people can't be wrong and they too panic. The bank is unable to produce the money its depositors demand. Obviously, most of the cash is invested or loaned. Within hours the bank is forced to close its doors and does indeed collapse. This example is hypothesized. Yet, many economists suggest this is precisely what occurred in the 1929 collapse.

The prophecy was a rumor of closure. By reacting to the rumor as if it were true, it became self-fulfilling. The phenomenon of self-fulfilling prophecy occurs daily. It is one of the most powerful of psychological principles, and it happens with both positive and negative results. In this book the term *Pygmalion effect* will be used interchangeably with self-fulfilling prophecy. I will show how to use these concepts to set up your children as winners.

_____

BELIEF EFFECT

All children could be winners but aren't. In fact, unfortunately, very few are. The balance is most often determined by the verbal and nonverbal messages they receive from the world around them and the environment at home. The messages can be intentional or unintentional, and sometimes they are communicated indirectly. However, they all have a major impact on how your children perceive the expectations you have for them.

I usually assume the best of people. Certainly, I did the first time I met Patrick's mother, Sandra. Like her son, Sandra was friendly and outgoing. They both were quick-witted and enjoyed jokes and puns. They looked alike. Both were large and powerfully built. Patrick described himself as Wisconsin-Norwegian, and he looked the part. His blond hair was bleached almost white from his outdoor activity. As his father before him, Patrick's hobbies were sailing in the summer and playing hockey in the winter. It was his way of life.

Like her sixteen-year-old son, Sandra was proud of her Norwegian heritage. However, she wasn't quite as proud of her son. It wasn't that she didn't love him. She did. And she was a good mother. But her belief system could not be suppressed. Sandra had been abandoned by Patrick's father two days after Patrick's birth. He subsequently married a family friend. Adding insult to injury, he had never financially supported her or Patrick. In fact, he stopped visiting after Patrick's third birthday. According to Sandra, Patrick's father was an alcoholic and a bum. When discussing him she spat the words out in a venomous baritone. "The jerk," she would announce. "He was such an idiot."

During these conversations, Patrick would stare blankly at the floor, appearing totally guilty and convicted. Sandra wasn't talking about him. She was referring to his biological father. But Patrick's entire personality seemed to change when Sandra went on one of these harangues. There was probably good reason. For years Patrick had heard people say, "You're just like your dad," or "You look just like your father," or make other similar references. Now his mother, in making critical comments about his father, was being indirectly critical of him. Her comments destroyed his self-worth. From one authoritative source he heard, "You're just like your father." And from another he heard, "Your father was scum." The logical conclusion for Patrick was that he had no personal value.

Sandra had assumed a belief system about Patrick's father. Later conversations revealed she had a similar attitude about her own father. It became clear that she had subconsciously transferred these same feelings to men in general. Though unaware of it, she communicated her condemning attitude to Patrick.

Patrick had been referred to me for two reasons. He had been caught driving while intoxicated, and he had gotten his girlfriend pregnant.

The words "He's just like his father" resounded in my ears.

Unfortunately, Patrick had become his mother's worst fear. He had become her belief. Sandra's belief system began as "my father is a jerk." Reinforced by her husband after marriage, it became "men who are close to me are jerks." And soon it evolved to "all men are jerks." Apparently Patrick was condemned for being male as well as for being "just like his father." In Patrick's case most of this was communicated implicitly. Sandra did indeed love her son. She would be described by most people as a "good mother." Her basic beliefs, nevertheless, could not be denied. And Patrick couldn't escape her expectations. He did indeed live up to them. He became "just like his father."

While preaching in Judea, Christ proclaimed, "Do to others what you would have them do to you, for this sums up the Law and the Prophets" (Matthew 7:12). Christ advocated a belief system that people are worthy of kindness, regardless of circumstances. At one point he suggested feeding the hungry, taking in the homeless, and visiting the sick and imprisoned. He declared that helping these people was the same as helping God himself.

Christ also seemed to suggest a belief system that did not respect labels, creeds, or colors, as the story of the Good Samaritan so aptly illustrates.

Yet, labels still get in the way. In Sandra's mind, the label of "just like his father" affected her perception of Patrick. In many ways labels affect us all.

HAWTHORNE EFFECT

One of the best known and earliest sociological studies that shows how labeling works was conducted at a Western Electric plant in Hawthorne, Indiana. The purpose of the consultant, Elton Mayo, was to see what changes could be made in the plant to increase productivity. The study, completed in the 1930s, was the first of its type. The results of the study changed the way people thought about the workplace.

A group of women workers were separated from others to take part in the study. They were told that this was a special experiment and that they had been chosen because of their reliability at work. Systematic changes were made in the workplace, and the researchers measured how the changes affected productivity. First, they changed the method of payment. Productivity went up! Next, they introduced brief rest periods. Production went up again. Next, they served refreshments twice a day. Production increased again. The researchers tried other changes, and productivity went up each time. Finally, the changes were all reversed. Production continued to climb. When the experiment ended, production went up again! The experimenters ended their study in disgrace. They believed they had failed.

There has been enormous speculation and discussion over the years as to what the Hawthorne experiment proved. Some say it simply demonstrated that people want to please experimenters and will try to help the experiment be a success. But I disagree.

The women in the Hawthorne studies felt special. They had been told how important the experiment was. They were chosen by management, who placed a great deal of confidence in them. This caused their self-confidence to soar. They had been identified as special. They received special treatment. And their belief in themselves was reflected in their productivity. The workers were flattered by the attention they received and as a result worked harder.

To me, the *Hawthorne effect* is actually the first controlled demonstration of the self-fulfilling prophecy. It was an example not only of the actual phenomenon but also of its power. If a person is treated as if he is important, his behavior will reflect that belief.

A cultural example of the *Hawthorne effect* is found in the Ashanti of Ghana, who name their children after the day of the week on which the child is born. A child born on Monday is called Kwadwo, the Ashanti name for Monday. However, used in another context, the same word means quiet, peaceful, and retiring. A child born on Wednesday is given the name Kwaku, the Ashanti name for that day of the week. Unfortunately, depending on the usage, it can also mean quick-tempered and aggressive.

Court records reveal that a majority of crimes among the Ashanti are committed by Kwakus. Anthropologists suggest the only factor that seems to have any effect on this phenomenon is the name itself! Parents expect children born on Wednesday to be violent. And that's what they become.

The *Hawthorne effect* works, and the process of labeling is frighteningly powerful. One fearsome aspect is that as adults, we are frequently placed in the position of applying labels. Equally as alarming is the response children make once given the label. Several years ago a friend's daughter suffered a severe back injury and had to be placed in a body cast, making it difficult for her to get in and out of school buses. In their community, a small van transported students who were handicapped. It came later than the regular bus, had wheelchair access, and other advantages the larger bus didn't.

Children have a way of being vicious to each other at times. They probably don't mean to be, and certainly they are incapable of realizing the potential consequences. Yet the damage they inflict can be severe. My friend found this out too late. The small van had been labeled "the retarded bus," and its inhabitants "retards." The label soon affected my friend's daughter. In reality, there were no retarded children riding in the van. But labels are more powerful than reality. His daughter's self-esteem plummeted. Her grades went down. She became sick and eventually refused to attend school. The label was more than she could bear both academically and emotionally.

Unfortunately, even kindergarten children are often overtly or covertly labeled and grouped into some category. The classifications flourish: retarded, learning-disabled, emotionally disturbed, hyperkinetic, brain dysfunctional, maladjusted, or simply slow learner. These children are then separated and often treated differently from others. Special classifications are perpetuated by other students, psychologists, or teachers who think the label is important.

The same effect can occur when a child is labeled troublemaker, problem child, or rebellious. Adults can easily respond to the label rather than the child. Your expectations become influenced by the label, and the child's behavior will usually follow these expectations. And even if the child's behavior doesn't match your expectations, the interpretation you make of their actions usually will. This was illustrated earlier by Rosenthal's research and later by other researchers.

Labeling can be an incredibly dangerous and powerful phenomenon, and damage caused by labeling in some cases is irreversible. But it can also have a positive and powerful effect. Research indicates that when teachers have a positive view of students' abilities, the students are likely to respond in a similarly positive direction. Children develop best in the presence of adults who see them as worthy, positive, and valuable. Holding the child in a position of high esteem will communicate more in a positive way than words ever will. Labeling works both ways. You can use the process to hurt or help your child.

PLACEBO EFFECT

I have worked in several drug rehabilitation centers across the country and with hundreds of people addicted to drugs. It was always sadly amusing when I heard these people explain that they weren't really physiologically addicted. I would tell them I wasn't really interested because, first, they were usually wrong, but more importantly, distinguishing between physiological and psychological addiction is not the important issue.

I have observed people take a completely empty syringe and pump it in and out of a vein. I have seen heroin addicts experience what they described as sexual excitement when they finally drew blood from their nearly collapsed veins. One addicted patient tried to kill another because he thought someone had stolen his empty syringe. He had been putting warm water in it and pumping it into his arm.

It is impossible for someone to get physiologically addicted to a needle. It is equally impossible for one to become addicted to water. However, we can become psychologically addicted to anything. It actually depends on the expectation. The expected outcome of an event is more important than the event itself. You can't get high with an empty needle. Or can you?

Various studies have been conducted to investigate the

placebo effect. The placebo effect occurs, as an example, when a patient gets better simply because he thinks something is being done for him. Most controlled studies impose a "double blind" effect, which means that neither the people taking part in the experiment nor the experimenter know full details of the study.

In one of these studies, both the physician giving medication and the patients receiving it thought they were getting medicine to treat high blood pressure. In reality, the treatment was a sugar pill. Yet, the patients' blood pressure lowered. It made no difference that they were receiving a placebo sugar pill.

Physiologically, a sugar pill cannot lower blood pressure, nor can a needle result in a sexual experience. But for some people they do. Similarly a person should not get high smoking ragweed. But if told that it's high grade marijuana, chances are he will.

All of these show that what a person believes can be more important than reality. Your expectations as a parent, teacher, or concerned adult will help determine a child's belief. Unlike the placebo, the effect of your expectations can be fatal. This was dramatically illustrated by my relationship with Tammy.

Tammy originally visited my office on referral from her gynecologist. Her parents had died in a tragic accident years before, and she suffered from chronic guilt related to their deaths. Her relationship with both parents had been very poor at the time of the accident. In fact, they were killed less than one hour after an argument with her. After several sessions, our visits concluded, and she went on with her life. Six months later she called in and reported that she was getting along okay.

"Still not pregnant, though," she said.

I had forgotten that this was an issue with Tammy. She had been trying to become pregnant for quite some time. Both she and her husband received every conceivable test and tried dozens of potions. Nothing seemed to help. As we spoke, I

remembered something from the personal history questionnaire she had filled out. I couldn't recall completely so I asked
her about it.

"Mother and I used to have these terrible fights. She was a
vegetarian and didn't like me to eat hamburgers and stuff. But I
hated vegetables. So I would eat junk food. Doughnuts,
hamburgers, and the like. I'm still a terrible eater."

"What was that one scene you described in your questionnaire? Didn't they force-feed you or something?"

"You've got a good memory. It was terrible. My dad would
wrap his arm around my neck and squeeze my mouth open
with his fingers. Then mother shoved those terrible vegetables
down my throat. It was awful. She used to tell me nobody
would like me if I didn't eat vegetables, that I'd never have any
friends, never date, the whole bit."

"Well, I'll tell you what we can do. You talk to your
husband tonight. See if he still wants to go through with this
pregnancy idea. He may have changed his mind. Babies really
change your life; I can assure you. That will give me time to
look over my notes. Seems like I remember something. But I
don't want to discuss it unless you're both sure."

It took me over an hour to go over her chart, but I found
what I thought was there. Tammy had written about her
memories of the forced feeding sessions. I had asked her to
write in detail everything she remembered her mother saying
to her about eating vegetables. What I had remembered was in
the middle of a paragraph. I had not even consciously noted it
in my earlier brief review. Apparently, she had no memory of
writing it either. I wondered if it had been an unconscious
projection of some sort. Perhaps she had written what she was
unable to say aloud. Before I had finished reading the material,
Tammy interrupted me with another phone call. She was
anxious to hear what I had to say.

I reminded Tammy she had said she'd try anything. Then I
persuaded her she had nothing to lose by trying my recommendation. After all, everything else had failed. Then I convinced

her I was certain that my idea would work, even though I wasn't. But I knew I had to sound persuasive before she would be convinced. This was one case where face-to-face conversation would not have worked. Nonverbal behavior would have given me away.

"Tammy," I paused for effect. "You don't need to see any more fertility experts to get pregnant. You've already been through all that. The experts say there's nothing wrong, but there is. They just didn't have all the facts.

"If you want to be pregnant, here's all you have to do. Just eat vegetables three days a week for a month, and then call me and tell me if you've done so. Then call me a month later and tell me you've eaten vegetables three days a week for two months in a row. During the same conversation you'll be able to tell me you're pregnant."

We spoke for a few more minutes. Then I got her husband on the phone and gave him the same information. They both thought it was a little silly! We all laughed and joked about my strategy, but she followed through and one month later told me she had eaten the vegetables as prescribed. Two months later she called again and said she had followed through, but still wasn't pregnant. I asked her specifically what vegetables she remembered being forced down her throat. She couldn't recall, but said they were "green and slimy." I suggested she try for one more month, but this time eat only green and slimy vegetables. She did. Within two weeks, she called and told me that she had actually been pregnant the second time she reported back, but didn't know it!

I didn't remind Tammy of one of the things she had written in her questionnaire. One of the things her mother had told her while force-feeding her was "If you don't eat vegetables, you'll never have a baby." Apparently, within weeks of that conversation her parents were killed unexpectedly.

Unknowingly, Tammy's mother had set a negative self-fulfilling prophecy into motion. It had been strengthened by her mother's premature death. It's not okay to prove your mother a liar. That's especially true if your mother is dead.

I'll never know why Tammy was able to get pregnant. It may have been coincidence. Perhaps, however, she was able to free herself from a very powerful unconscious sanction that had set up a negative self-fulfilling prophecy. Whatever the truth was, her pregnancy was a result. Neither she nor I will ever know for sure. But she still eats vegetables! And today she has two children!

WINNER

A winner is a child who is emotionally healthy and has a proper balance of self-confidence and belief in her ability to succeed. The winner attempts to fulfill her God-given potential. Winners such as these are made, not born. There are certain things you can do to assist your child in becoming this kind of winner. An example can be found in a small rural school district outside Charlotte, North Carolina.

Several years ago I conducted a seminar on the Pygmalion concept for elementary school teachers. One second grade teacher grew quite excited and wondered aloud how she could apply it to the children entering her class that fall. We discussed it in great detail, and then I more or less forgot about her.

Several months ago I received a very enthusiastic letter from this teacher. She had not only used the Pygmalion effect, she had used it very successfully.

After our discussion on the day of the seminar, she decided on a plan. On the opening day of class, she met each child at the door. Kneeling on one knee, she whispered privately to each one.

"You probably don't know this," she began, "but you've got to be real smart to get in my grade. Only the extra-smart boys and girls get to be in here. But don't tell anybody. It will be our secret."

The children's eyes lit up in disbelief. "Really?" they asked. "Just wait till I tell Mommy and Daddy!" Then they went to find one of their young friends already seated.

"Are you extra-smart too?" they exclaimed. "I didn't know you were smart enough for this grade."

Soon she started getting phone calls from surprised parents. Not knowing what to say, she convinced them that their children were indeed "extra-smart!" It worked. That year attendance soared. The following year she used the Pygmalion effect again, with similar results.

The Pygmalion effect works equally well with children and adults. Rosenthal discovered this years ago after a nearly identical experiment. Participants were divided into two groups and directed to watch identical movies of a normal first-grade class. One group was told that the first graders were in an advanced gifted class and to look for signs of giftedness. The other group was informed that the students were in a special class of learning disabled and hyperactive children and to look for signs of learning disabilities.

After watching the movie, the participants were able to list several dozen examples of what they were motivated to find. The "gifted" group found nothing but gifted behavior. The other group found nothing but evidence of learning disability and hyperactivity. Yet both groups saw the same movie!

Several years later Rosenthal moved from his laboratory setting into an actual elementary classroom. This time he appeared to be working in an official capacity with the school district, and with the cooperation of the teachers. After testing the entire classroom of students, Rosenthal chose the most average of students and convinced the teachers that these particular students would excel in the coming year, and in fact, were intellectually gifted.

At the completion of the school year Rosenthal found his "gifted" children had indeed excelled. The teachers unfailingly described this group as having fewer behavior problems, less absenteeism, and making higher grades than other students. After being informed that the students were actually chosen at random and in fact were average, the teachers were surprised. They were shocked later to discover that the children randomly designated by Rosenthal as gifted, increased their IQ scores by as much as seven points more than those not receiving the false designation.

There is no explanation to describe specifically what occurred with Rosenthal's experimentation. Somehow the teachers' expectations were communicated to their students. This was apparently done more nonverbally than verbally. The teachers honestly did believe their students were going to excel. Their belief was powerful enough that, as with Liza Doolittle, it began to rub off. The students were set up as winners.

Of course, the same effect can occur in reverse. Several years ago one of my colleagues tested a teenager for me. The teenager had actually done quite well on the testing, and my colleague gladly gave him the news that he scored above the 90th percentile for intelligence. This means that over 90 percent of those who took the test scored lower than this young man. He was therefore in the top ten percent of those who took the test. An equivalent IQ score would be in the range of 130–140. My colleague said one thing, but what the teenager and his parents heard was that he had an IQ of 90! There was a huge difference.

I saw this teenager several times afterward in counseling. We discussed the testing, and I complimented his performance. He must have thought I was confused. Months later I received a phone call from his mother. "I don't guess we should say anything about his grades being down, should we?" his mother asked.

"I don't know. I didn't know they were going down." My mind began searching for a reason why Jim's grades would drop. He had already been through the preadolescent letdown; so it wasn't that.

"Well, ever since that other doctor told him his IQ was 90,

that was. Being singled out and made different than everyone else was awful. My friends stayed away from me like I was contagious. People called me names. I got to the point I hated school. So I quit going.

"I really don't know what would have happened. But I remember it like yesterday. I just wasn't going to go back. My parents, thank God, were sensitive people. They supported me and seemed to really care about everything that was happening.

"What I didn't know was that we were getting ready to move. This had probably gone on two months after I was put in the special class. Well, I don't know if I was a slow learner or not before I started the class. But I sure was after being put in there. The teacher didn't seem to care. The other kids were as bored as I was. You could not imagine what it was like. We were being babysat, not taught.

"So, I decided I wouldn't go back. Then we moved. At first I didn't want to go to school at all. I don't know if it was a foul-up or not, but they put me in a normal class. I don't even think there was a special class at the new school. Anyway, I got a teacher that just loved me to death. She used to call me up at home on Saturdays and get me to come over to the school to help her fix bulletin boards. She made me feel special in a good way.

"Soon I got excited about school, made wonderful grades the rest of my life, and then went to college and graduate school. And it was all because of this one woman who took an interest in me.

"But what would have happened had it not been for her? Where would I be today? That's really frightening to me. Labels can be fatal."

IMPROVING YOUR PARENTING ART

1. Study your own level of self-confidence. Consider at what point in your life it was highest. Lowest. Do you recall any occasion when you accomplished something because someone believed in you more than you did in yourself? How did that feel? How did it affect your level of self-confidence?

2. Consider the behavior of your own children. Do they act like "winners" or "losers?" Discuss with them how they feel about themselves as well as their expectations of themselves.

3. Examine your own expectations and beliefs about your children. Determine if there are any differences in what you *want* of them and what you *expect* of them. Begin observing your own verbal and nonverbal communications with your children. Do these reflect messages that will help set them up as "winners?" Repeat often the positive verbal and nonverbal messages of expectation that your children are winners.

PARENTING EXERCISES

1. Find out from your children, through discussion and listening, how others act toward them and what names or labels may have been placed on them. Encourage them to talk about their feelings.

2. Examine the different areas of your child's environment such as home, neighborhood, school, church, and activities. What factors do you find that will help set your child up to be a winner? What factors do you find that will help set her up to be a loser?

3. Take action to help eliminate the negative factors and increase the positive factors by discussing your findings with teachers, pastors, friends, family members, and other significant adults in your child's life.

The brightest expression of civilization is not its art, but the supreme tenderness that people are strong enough to feel and show toward one another.

—*Norman Cousins*

Love your neighbor as yourself. All the Law and the Prophets hang on these two commandments.

—*Matthew 22:39–40*

4

Bring Out the Best
in Your Child

I HAD NEVER babysat for Jeffrey before. His parents and I were good friends and on several occasions Jeffrey and I had played together. However, this was the first time for him to stay with me for any extended period. Normally, we had gotten along quite well. He was an extremely bright four-year-old and usually very cooperative.

During the time he stayed with me, Jeffrey had a daily allowance of two dollars. He used the money to play video games, buy sweets, or go to movies. This particular day we stopped by a grocery store so that I could do some shopping. I was getting ready to go through the checkout line when Jeffrey found a toy truck he wanted to purchase. I told him that was fine; but since the truck cost $1.79, he wouldn't be able to play the video games and also purchase the truck.

"I want both," he demanded. "I want the truck and to play video games." He looked at me defiantly.

Even though I was teaching college classes in child

psychology, I had little actual experience with young children. So, I attempted reasoning with him. I figured I simply wasn't getting through.

"No, Jeffrey, you don't seem to understand. You've only got two dollars. If you spend all this money on your truck, you'll have nothing left. Video games are a quarter each. You won't even have a quarter, so you can't do both." There, I thought to myself. That should make sense to him.

Jeffrey glared. "I want both!" he demanded. "I want the truck and the video games!"

I began again to explain but was interrupted by what I thought was a shriek of pain. "Jeffrey, what's wrong?" I was scared he was hurt.

"No. I want both." And for the first time, I got to observe a bona fide foot-stomping temper tantrum. He closed his eyes, balled his fists, and screeched until his cheeks were purple!

This presented me with an interesting challenge. As Professor Baucom, the "expert," I had spoken to countless students and parent groups on dealing with tantrums, but this was my first real life experience.

My mind raced. Here we are in a grocery store aisle, surrounded by other shoppers. This child is screaming like I've abused him. People are scowling at me, accusedly. I've got to do something.

What now, Doctor?

STROKING

Some time ago my eldest son and I were shooting basketballs into his miniature goal. I normally applaud or give my children a great deal of praise when they succeed. This time was no exception. Since he is a good shot, we stopped often for applause. After a few minutes he reached into his toy box and withdrew a page of miniature "stick on" happy faces. I watched as he began to shoot the ball. Quickly, he got one through the basket. After applauding his own success, he calmly placed the ball down on the floor and reached into his pocket. He removed one of the happy face stickers and placed it on his forearm. Ignoring me, he shot another through the hoop, applauded himself, and repeated the happy face procedure. Then he repeated it a third time. Before the game was over, he had fourteen happy faces covering his left forearm!

I give a large number of stickers (or strokes) to my children. I believe that rewarding people with social recognition is an important part of any relationship. I want my children to grow up with self-confidence and a strong belief in their ability to achieve. So I give them positive reinforcement. What my son illustrated was a very important process. He showed that no longer was he totally dependent on me for his own self-esteem. Now, as demonstrated, he could give strokes to himself.

A stroke doesn't necessarily have to be a happy face. Many high school and college football teams use different forms of strokes. Instead of Ohio State football helmets being plastered with happy faces, they get miniature buckeyes stuck on their helmets. The stickers are based on individual and team performance. Clemson players get miniature tiger paws. Other teams use miniature footballs or other token decals.

A stroke in its best form is something other than a decal. It can be any response to any behavior. Smiling at your child, saying thank you, hugging them, or patting them on the back can all be positive strokes. These strokes have a tremendous impact on behavior and morale as well. Children whose lives are rewarded with social recognition will usually be more productive and reliable than those who aren't. These are bold claims, but the claims are no more powerful than strokes are if properly given. And that's not a claim at all. It's a statement of fact supported by years of research as well as by experience. My first exposure to positive reinforcement came quite early.

After my father's death, I lost interest in many things, including school. For three years in a row, I made barely passing grades. The years prior, I had been a consistent straight-A student. Accompanying this decline were the normal types of adjustment problems any ten-year-old would suffer from such a tragedy. One of these problems was jealousy of people my mother dated. I'm certain she refused several marriage proposals because of my reactions. Finally, however, she remarried.

My stepfather, Jack, was a "mountain man" and a commercial farmer. He didn't have the advantage or limitations of a formal education and probably was wiser without it. He had never raised children, nor had he taken a psychology class, but he obviously knew something about motivation. After looking at my first report card, Jack decided to take action. He didn't yell, scream, or beat me up. I have no idea why he used the approach he did. But it worked.

"John, Son. Tell you what let's do," he drawled. "These grades here just aren't right. So let's make us a deal. For an *A* I'll give you three dollars. For a *B* I'll give you two dollars. For a *C* we'll break even. But for a *D* you pay me two dollars, and for an *F* you pay me three. How does that sound?"

It was the best offer I'd had in years! This was back in the days when three dollars was a lot of money. It was also in the days when you used to get ten or twelve grades each reporting period!

I don't know what Jack expected to happen. But in one grading period I went from all *D*s and *F*s to *A*s and *B*s! Jack ended up forking over twenty-six dollars for that report card! He was shocked, but he never backed out of the deal! My grades never went down again. At first my motivation was money, not school. But I had to study to make the grades. Eventually I became excited about learning, although it took some time. For the rest of my academic life, including high school, college, and graduate school, I never made anything below a *B*. Jack probably didn't understand the concept of positive reinforcement. Nevertheless, he intuitively knew how to bring out the best in me when it came to grades.

SHAPING

Strokes are one of the most powerful ways to shape behavior. We define shaping as any pleasant response to a behavior that tends to strengthen that behavior. In a laboratory experiment, feeding a rat for pressing a bar is reinforcing the rat's behavior. Smiling and talking to an infant for trying to walk is reinforcing the walking. Complimenting the cook for a good meal is reinforcing the cook. Through elaborate positive reinforcement systems pigeons have been taught to play ping pong and the piano. Orangutans and chimpanzees have been taught sign language. Dolphins have been taught to locate submarines and lost scuba divers. Many people respond just as powerfully.

Many years ago as a college student, I had the opportunity to experiment with these principles. Some students used pigeons for their experiments, others used rats, and others used people. I had an opportunity to work with all three. People, by far, were the most interesting. I did very little original experimentaton. Nevertheless, I enjoyed hearing of attempts former researchers had made and then doing similar experiments myself.

On several experiments a group of us collaborated to see if we could change peoples' behavior through using a simple kind of positive reinforcement. On one project we complimented a particular girl every time she wore something green. We never criticized her for wearing any other color. We simply told her she looked nice every time she wore something green. Three days after we began she wore a green dress. Exactly three weeks later she wore green leotards, green bows in her hair, and green shoes! This change in dress resulted only from compliments (strokes/reinforcement) for wearing that color.

On another occasion we decided to see if we could influence our professor. This was a rather difficult challenge, because he had told us about doing the same thing when he was a student. But we figured if positive reinforcement was so powerful, it couldn't fail. So we tried it. When he stood on the right side of the podium, we smiled and tried to look interested. When he stood on the left side, we yawned and looked bored. After twenty minutes he was lecturing only from the right side of the podium. Before class was over, he figured out what we were doing. But it worked.

Many years later a class I was teaching did an almost identical thing to me. They changed it around so that the only time they paid attention was when I sat on a table in front of the classroom. I sat there for fifteen minutes before I realized what was happening. Through all this experimentation with people, pigeons, rats, and other primates, I quickly learned one thing. Most animals respond to food as a primary reinforcer. But with people, social attention is by far the most powerful kind of stroke.

IGNORING

Janice was both physically and emotionally emaciated. Her cadaverous soul was as hollow as the cavernous blank stare in her eyes. Her eighty-five pounds stretched tightly over her five-foot-six-inch frame. Unlike the majority of anorectics, Janice was in her midforties. What she had in common with others was an obsessive preoccupation with her body.

"I need to lose a few more pounds. I'm still too fat," she whined. "I weighed ten times yesterday. I was afraid I'd gained a pound." I ignored Janice when she discussed her obsession with weight. Apparently, I was the only person who did.

Although still married, the relationship she had with her husband was poor. Her children had grown up and left home. She had never worked outside her home and had few friends. She had done nothing to establish her own identity other than being a mother. When the children left, so did her sense of purpose.

Shortly after her last child was gone, Janice had a

hysterectomy. Weeks later, she entered long-term psychoanalysis four days a week with a psychiatrist. Approximately one year later, she began getting severe migraine headaches. As the migraines worsened, she visited a physician to treat them. Later she was convinced by a dentist that she had TMJ (tempormandibular joint pain) and began getting treatment to align her jaw. She also found out she had hypoglycemia and microvalve prolapse. Daily visits to her physician and four visits a week to her psychiatrist became common. The sicker she seemed to be, the more attention she received. After three years, the psychoanalyst terminated her treatment. That was when she became anorectic.

Her daughter returned home to help out after Janice began losing significant weight. Her husband, daughter, and a few friends constantly harped about weight and food. It almost became a game. The more weight she lost, the more attention she received. Janice had not been given this much attention her entire life. She felt important. She had become special. As an anorectic, she had identity but was locked into a downward spiral. Her thinking patterns were affected. Reality and fantasy merged. Eventually, after hospitalization, months of family therapy, and tremendous effort, Janice recovered. The key for her was learning a more positive identity and different ways to receive strokes.

Any behavior that is reinforced will be strengthened. A behavior that is ignored will be weakened. It's logical, then, to reward your child for desirable behavior and, when possible, ignore negative behavior. I give this advice to nearly all parents I meet in counseling sessions, conferences, or seminars. We easily and quickly respond when we catch our children doing something wrong. Most often, the proper or appropriate behavior goes ignored.

One of the primary principles of this chapter is that behavior responded to will be strengthened. Behavior ignored will eventually disappear. Perhaps this is why we so often see desirable behavior diminish among children. They don't get enough "happy faces" for it. To bring out the best in your children, stroke them for doing things *right*. You will then observe their desirable behavior being repeated time and time again. A six-year-old friend of mine stated it rather poetically.

Kevin was probably the cutest, red-haired six-year-old I had ever seen. Some people described him as feisty. Others said he was immature. His teacher called him unmanageable. I didn't find him to be any of those things and particularly objected to anyone labeling a six-year-old as immature. His family's visit to my office was triggered by Kevin's inability to concentrate on school work or sit still at school. He was constantly bringing home notes from the teacher telling what he had done wrong that day. Gradually, we implemented several of the strategies discussed in this book, and Kevin began to adapt. Basically, we focused on bringing out the best by patiently using a positive reinforcement system. Over time the program worked.

Several months later I got a phone call from his mother. She reported Kevin had gone over six weeks without bringing home a bad note from the teacher. The night before, she commented to Kevin about his progress. "Yeah," he replied. "But did you notice she never gives me a note when I do something good? It's only if I get in trouble. You ought to tell Dr. B about that!"

The teacher was making a tremendous mistake by not attending to Kevin's positive behavior the same way she had his negative behavior. Unfortunately, it's a mistake we, as adults, constantly make. To bring out the best, is to focus attention on desirable behavior and ignore that which is negative. There is a great deal of power in ignoring. This same principle applies to all people. Nothing hurts like being ignored. In a recent conversation with a former Vietnam prisoner of war this idea was poignantly supported. He explained the pain and actual horror of solitary confinement: "After a few days of confinement in a monkey cage, I would try to get someone to beat me or something. After awhile it was

Terry grew so depressed that her personal appearance and habits were affected. She attempted to escape through sleep.

Shortly thereafter, her parents decided Terry was possessed by demons. They contacted several ministers to exorcise the evil spirits. Terry responded with a spiraling depression and quickly entered what appeared to be a complete withdrawal from reality. This only convinced her parents that she was indeed possessed by demons. When Terry quit eating, a relative finally became involved. While her parents were away, Terry's aunt took her to a hospital emergency room. A physician there found Terry to be in dangerously poor health. She was immediately hospitalized and fed intravenously for several days. Later she was transferred to a psychiatric unit. Her parents refused to cooperate in treatment, so Terry was committed to the hospital against her parents' will.

Both Tommy and Terry eventually got the help they needed to survive. I believe their parents meant well and had the best of intentions. After interviewing all of them, it was clear they thought they were helping. In my opinion, had these parents learned to give affirming strokes, their children would never have experienced such trauma. Giving a positive stroke is very easy. It's much easier than suffering the consequences of not doing so.

RECOGNIZING

The principles of bringing out the best are extremely simple. First of all, the focus is on behavior. Some experts suggest observing closely and rewarding the child for reaching the behavioral goal (such as making the bed, picking up clothes, and being ready on time). The reward can be verbal and social or objective, such as points or tokens. By far, the most effective in my own professional experience is social and verbal reward.

It's important to tell the child specifically what he or she has done well and why such behavior is appreciated. Vague generalities, such as "You're such an angel," are inaccurate overgeneralizations and will be recognized as such by the child. In fact, such comments are embarrassing to most children. You can improve your child's self-image and self-confidence by indicating a specific act and describing to the child how it was helpful. The stroke is most effective if based on the child's behavior and not the child's personality. Examples include:

"Thanks for picking up the toys in your room, Josh. That gives Mom more time to play with you."

"Katie, I really appreciate your helping me with the dishes. That helps a lot and now I have more time to read to you."

There is another kind of stroke that is best described as a stroke for "being." It is based on the fact that the child is valuable and worthy just because he or she is alive and is your child. This is a message of unconditional value.

"You know, Josh, I'm proud to be your mom."

"Katie, I enjoy being your mom. I'm glad we have the same last name. You're a special little girl to me."

All of these strokes are powerful and important. They will help your child flourish. The use of strokes is not limited to school-aged children. It can also be used with toddlers, adults, and anyone else. Strokes have been used to increase the academic performance of mentally retarded children, to help cure people suffering from eating disorders such as anorexia nervosa, to help adults learn to control self-destructive impulses, to help people control heroin addictions, to improve reading skills, to help children learn bladder and bowel control, and for hundreds of other purposes. It is not a cure-all or panacea. However, properly used, strokes can help parents channel behavior while improving the self-esteem of children.

Specifically, what you do to bring out the best in the children of your life depends on their unique personalities. Most children who are not suffering from emotional damage will respond extremely well, and quite quickly, to affirming behaviors. Some teenagers who have grown alienated from authority figures take much longer to respond. If the adolescent is extremely alienated or angry, he will occasionally do just the opposite of what you, as an authority figure, reinforce! In these cases you must return to the process of building trust through spending meaningful time and showing love and acceptance. Eventually, the adolescent will overcome his anger and cynicism. Fortunately, these cases are in the minority. The majority of children respond exceptionally well to affirming behaviors.

It's very important to stroke small positive attempts and gradual improvements in behavior. As an example, it's important that young babies learn to walk. Initially, you praise the child for crawling and then scooting around in a walker. Eventually the child begins to hang onto the couch and take a few steps. You applaud this progress and tell her how great it is. Then she takes a few more steps and receives more praise. Soon, the child is walking on her own. Part of the responsibility belongs to the parent for praising gradual improvement. If the parents had waited for the child to take ten steps in a row before giving any reinforcement she may never have walked. As long as the behavior is going in the right direction, strengthen it with a stroke.

Some children require special kinds of reinforcement. George is a good example. He was in an institution for multiply handicapped children and had lived there virtually his entire life. George was functionally handicapped from multiple birth defects. He was severely mentally retarded, autistic, and microcephalic. He barely walked or responded, but by age thirteen he was large and strong. Unintentionally, he had injured several staff members.

Probably because of my size, I was asked to work one-on-one with George for six to eight hours per day in a behavioral training program. Initially, the progress was very slow as we got to know each other. George was suspicious of me and wouldn't trust easily. I experimented to find out what rein-

forced and affirmed George. Simple compliments didn't work.
Handshakes were meaningless. He wouldn't know what to do
with a token. As a result of his autism, hugs were ineffective or
meaningless. He did like to eat, though. So I decided to try
food.

The classic food reinforcer is M & M's. George liked them,
but he would never put them in his mouth. He always stuffed
them in his ear or nose. I tried other foods and eventually
settled on his favorite fruit, a banana. As he exhibited desirable
behavior, I would give him a bite of banana. Soon I decided to
help him learn different tasks. Each time he mastered a task I
would give him another banana. This process continued for
several weeks. Yet our relationship remained superficial.

One morning as I came in, he ran to meet me for the first
time. Since George had never demonstrated affection, I was
very confused. I shrugged my shoulders to ask what he was
doing. He lowered his head and staggered into my open arms.
He began to hug me while humming! I was so excited I picked
George up off the floor and began to carry the large teenager
around. In response, he wrapped his arms around my neck and
snuggled into my chest!

From that time on, we became a spectacle at the institution. Quite by mistake I discovered the other way to bring out
the best in George. Each day for a minimum of thirty minutes, I
would carry him in my arms with his arms around my neck.
When he accomplished tasks in his learning program, I picked
him up and swung him around. He would smile and eventually laugh. Bananas lost their reinforcing power. Like the rest
of us, George desired social strokes. He was affirmed.

*I was in a dilemma with Jeffrey. I believe that you get what
you stroke. If I gave in to his tantrum, I would be teaching him
you can get whatever you want from life by having tantrums. I
would also be teaching Jeffrey he can control other peoples'
behavior by being irrational. That would be an extremely
dangerous lesson. If I gave in, both Jeffrey and I would lose.*

On the other hand, spanking him or raising my voice could be equally destructive. I would be giving Jeffrey attention, even though adverse, that probably would still strengthen the behavior. I would also be modeling aggressiveness. I needed to remove the motive for his tantrum. Rather than embarrassing me into buying a toy, I needed to place the focus on him. Instead of begging him to stop his behavior, which would give him power, I needed to allow him to choose. I wanted to remove the audience that his behavior was meant to influence, and provide Jeffrey with a way out of the dilemma. Instead of learning he can get what he wants by acting crazy, I wanted him to learn you get more attention by being healthy.

"Jeffrey, wait a minute," I interrupted. "Hang on just a minute. Let's talk." As Jeffrey began to calm from the tantrum, I turned to some of the people around me.

"Hi," I began. "Excuse me, this is Jeffrey. He is not my child, and I am not his dad. I'm babysitting for him today. He has decided to put on a show. If you'd like to watch, please feel free to, but I'm going to go on with my shopping."

I'm not sure who was the most startled. It all happened so quickly. But from the looks on their faces, the other shoppers were even more surprised than I was.

"Oh, Jeffrey!" I turned around. "You can come with me or you can stay here and have tantrums. Either way is okay. I'm just bored by that kind of stuff." And I walked away.

Without hesitating Jeffrey walked toward me, leaving the shoppers in the aisle staring at us both. "I think I'd rather go play video games," he quickly commented. And that's what we did without discussing the issue further.

Jeffrey has never had another tantrum.

IMPROVING YOUR PARENTING ART

1. Think about your attitudes toward your child or children. When do you give them the greatest and most intense attention? What happens following your interactions with them?

2. Looking back to your own childhood, which of your actions, whether acceptable or unacceptable, were stroked the most by adults? What got more attention, negative or positive behavior?

3. How have you stroked your children? Did it help? If not, what would you do differently?

PARENTING EXERCISES

1. Try an experiment with your child. Ignore unacceptable behavior for two weeks.

2. Try another experiment. Choose an acceptable behavior and for thirty days make a conscious attempt to reinforce it.

GOOD TIMES!

Let us not love with words or tongue but with actions and in truth. . . . And this is his command: to believe in the name of his Son, Jesus Christ, and to love one another as he commanded us.

—*1 John 3:18, 23*

O divine Master, grant that I may not so much seek to be consoled as to console; to be understood as to understand; to be loved as to love. For it is in giving that we receive; it is in pardoning that we are pardoned. . . .

—*St. Francis of Assisi*

5

Pay Attention to
Your Child

ANDY WAS nearly twenty when he graduated from high
school. The fact he graduated at all was a miracle. He needed
more than most children.

I had never really responded emotionally at a high school
graduation. But this was not a normal ceremony. This was
Andy's graduation. And Andy was not just any high school
senior. Everyone had given up on Andy except his adopted
family. It took work to get him placed with the Cox family.
There were complications nobody could have predicted. But
with the help of several compassionate social workers, an
aggressive attorney, and at substantial expense, he finally
made it.

As a child, Andy was considered severely mentally
retarded. He was one of those infants you read about in the
newspaper and shake your head in disbelief. A policeman
discovered Andy, only days old, wrapped in several blankets
inside a huge trash dumpster. The policeman was cleaning his

squad car out and heard cries coming from the trash. Nobody ever discovered who his parents were or where he came from. Apparently, his early infancy was marked by serious illness, and he spent months in and out of different hospitals.

When I met Andy, he was nine years old and in a state facility for multiply handicapped, mentally retarded children. My life was never the same after our relationship began. Had I known I would ultimately lose my job as a result of that relationship, perhaps my attitude would have been different. But I doubt it.

TOO MUCH ATTENTION

Your children need attention. Substantial evidence shows that tremendous positive changes can occur when children are given a balance of appropriate attention. Paradoxically, people in today's world, including most children, don't get enough of it.

The quality of attention is not such that it is overinvolved or overprotective. At the same time, it is not one that is detached and underinvolved. There is a balance of closeness and separateness. Far too often we see the extremes of children not getting any attention from their parents or the overly involved parent who doesn't allow the child to develop a separate identity. Both ends of the spectrum have led to severe emotional difficulty for all family members.

Each member of a family needs to have separate, personal boundaries. These are invisible, but distinct lines that separate one person from another. Often parents appear to be gaining selfish gratification through a child's achievement. Other times a parent almost lives her life through her child. On other occasions a child may play the role of "surrogate spouse," in place of the physically or emotionally absent parent. In all of these cases, the child is definitely getting attention. Unfortunately, it's not of a healthy quality. The balance is elusive and too often we find it's more troublesome counterparts. A disturbing example of imbalance occurred in the family of a friend.

The visit with my friend Bob had gone well. This was the first time I had seen him since his hospitalization. We had been friends for a couple of years. My visit to the hospital was a social one. I don't recall how we originally met. We didn't have a lot in common, but he seemed to enjoy my family. He was a very athletic, out-spoken young man in his early twenties and had been a frequent visitor at our home. Often, he was there before I returned in the evenings, playing soccer with my children, and giving Bennie a much deserved rest. We grew close as friends, but I was aware our relationship lacked depth. I knew almost nothing of his family background. It didn't seem important at the time. He was fine as he was.

I eventually met Bob's girlfriend, Angie, and she too became another regular houseguest. We were all able to get along well in spite of the age differences. I don't recall any discussion of emotional or family problems. Certainly, I regarded Bob as different than most people his age. Maybe he was a bit eccentric, but I appreciated that quality in him.

On a Friday evening in December, I received a phone call. "Bob just tried to kill himself. It's real bad. Can you meet us at the emergency room?"

"Angie, is this you?" I didn't know what to say.

"Yeah, I'm sorry John," she cried.

"Okay, which emergency room?"

I rushed to the nearby hospital and saw Bob being rolled out of the ambulance. He wore a body compression suit and had lost a tremendous amount of blood from a deep laceration to his throat. Angie was close behind the ambulance. Two older adults arrived. I assumed they were Bob's parents. Paramedics gave medical information. I realized how little I knew this friend. I couldn't give his blood type or even his birth date. I was of no assistance and wondered how I could help.

Bob's father introduced himself. In our brief discussion that evening I was able to piece together a bit of the puzzle. Bob had come home from a date with Angie several hours late. Although he was twenty-three years old, his parents still kept Bob on a curfew. (He had never even told me he lived at home!) An argument ensued that became extremely volatile. They told him that he could no longer see Angie, and they made other demands. At this point, Bob ran into the bathroom and, after struggling with his father, cut his own throat.

Bob's father blamed Angie and explained that the entire scenario was her fault. "We didn't have any problem until she came around. He used to stay home more." After visiting Angie and checking with the physicians, I left the emergency room. They assured me he would recover. Two days later they transferred him out of intensive care.

My visit with Bob that day was encouraging. It was difficult to believe that he had attempted suicide only a few days before. While Angie sat at his side, I stood at the foot of the bed. We laughed while discussing the "Doonesbury" comic strip for the day. There was a knock on the door. His parents entered, embraced Bob, and stood opposite Angie. Bob seemed glad to see them and smiled. They didn't notice me, so I backed away from the bed.

"Here, Son," his father said. "I brought you a Twinkie." He placed his offering on the bedside table. The conversation continued a few minutes longer.

"Bob, here—eat your Twinkie, Son. They're not feeding you enough." His father pushed the snack cake toward his son who ignored it the second time. The conversation continued. Angie joined in as they all discussed the football games of that weekend. A few minutes later Bob's father picked up the Twinkie and literally shoved it under his son's twenty-three-year-old nose.

"Bob, please, Son. Eat your Twinkie. You've been losing weight. You need to eat," he pleaded.

I would mortgage my house to have a video tape of what

happened next. Bob's reaction was the most dramatic example of the psychological "double bind" I have ever seen demonstrated. As his father held the Twinkie under Bob's nose, Angie jerked it from Mr. Brown's hand. She turned her attention to Bob and smashed the Twinkie on his nightstand.

"If you want to eat the darn thing, go ahead! If you don't, just throw it away!" Angie glared sternly at Mr. Brown as she spoke. Although her words were accepting, the message was not. It was a clear challenge—to Mr. Brown more than to Bob. The moment was frozen for an uncomfortable fifteen seconds.

Bob's response was classic. He was stuck in a double bind from which there was no escape. If he ate the Twinkie, he lost. Angie would be upset. If he didn't eat the Twinkie, he lost. Father would be upset. Bob did the only logical thing he could do. He sank into his bed and pulled the pillow over his head. I'm certain he would have shot himself that moment if he could have.

After that interaction, Bob's condition worsened, and he entered a deep depressive state. I later learned he had been in and out of serious depressive episodes since junior high school. Over a year later, I worked with Bob's family in therapy. Bob was the youngest of four children and the only one at home. It became clear that his parents were experiencing tremendous difficulty letting Bob leave home and he was having difficulty getting the strength to do it on his own. Neither he nor his parents were equipped to handle his departure. Additionally, Bob's three siblings had not lived up to their parents' expectations. The parents seemed to have invested all of their hopes, dreams, and energy into Bob. In their minds it was the last opportunity for them to salvage part of their family. The pressure was obviously more than Bob could handle. After years of intense counseling, Bob was able to develop his own identity and leave home. It was a most painful move.

Today, Bob is a high-school football coach. He and Angie are married and have children of their own. He has unfortunately never rebuilt a healthy relationship with his parents. Bob's parents were overinvolved. They were dependent on Bob remaining at home, and that unintentionally created problems.

I have never met a parent with bad intentions. But good intentions do not necessarily build healthy parent-child relationships. A balance of nurture and recognition of separateness can help insure a relationship of health. And as being overinvolved can be emotionally unhealthy for your child, the same is also true of the opposite extreme.

TOO LITTLE ATTENTION

Joe was proud of his BMW. It had been a gift from his parents and grandparents who owned a large business, but he was more concerned about the direction of his life. He had come, on his own initiative, for individual counseling. That fact alone is extraordinary for someone his age. With his mother's permission, he called and made the appointment himself.

He was talkative during the sessions. It was one of the most unusual counseling cases I have ever experienced with a sixteen-year-old. Most people his age are hauled into counseling centers, against their will, by parents. They refuse to speak the first few sessions. You have to spend a great deal of time simply building rapport. But it was uniquely different with Joe. He was very mature and cooperative. He had few complaints about his life. His self-esteem was fine. No depression. Grades were excellent. He had a nice girlfriend.

"I'm just not close to my dad," Joe explained. "I seldom if ever see him. He travels all the time. I know I'm missing out on a lot, but I'm not sure what it is. I have never had anything to compare it with. Love is more than a BMW, you know?"

Joe had refocused me on the importance of emotional warmth and the significance of the parent-child relationship.

That very bond is vital, even if you are sixteen and do have your own BMW. Joe had never been abused or neglected in any way. His father simply wasn't there. Quite frankly, it took over a full year to get Joe's father into counseling. But in time, he did begin spending time with his son. Joe is now in college, and he spends a three-day weekend together with his father per month. Their relationship is stronger, and so is Joe.

Too little attention, like too much attention, is seldom the plan of most parents. More often it occurs as a result of well-intentioned parents whose responsibilities and time are spread too thinly. As a result, they have neither the time nor the energy to build a quality, well-balanced relationship with their children. The superficial quality of the parent-child relationship then becomes subtly abusive. Unfortunately, the emotional bruises are often unrecognized until it's almost too late to respond.

JUST THE RIGHT ATTENTION

The late Abraham Maslow was a brilliant psychologist and author. His work was not sufficiently understood at the time of his premature death in 1970. Today, he is recognized worldwide for his insight as well as for his contributions to the understanding of human behavior. Although Maslow did not direct his comments exclusively toward understanding children, his hierarchy of needs is certainly applicable to them.

One of Maslow's theories was that people are motivated to satisfy five different levels of needs. Each level must be satisfied consecutively. You cannot go to level four without satisfying levels one, two, and three. The first level encompassed "survival," or biological needs. These include food, air, water, and the like. Only after these needs are satisfied can progress be made to the second level—the need for "safety and security." This includes such things as shelter, clothing, food, and security from physical danger. The first two levels deal with survival or basic needs. Both must be met before the child can progress to meet the third level—the need for "love and belonging." At this level the child can form the basis for some degree of productivity or output. In turn, these needs are vital as a link to the fourth level—the need for "self-esteem." The fifth level is the need for "self-realization," or the need to develop one's potential and become more creatively productive. It is not surprising that the needs for love and belonging must be met before the needs for self-esteem and self-achievement. It illustrates the unique importance social attention has on personal, intellectual, and even biological development. Parental attention is a necessary building block for emotional growth and development.

Occasionally, safety and security needs are met, but love and belonging needs are not because of lack of parental attention. Interesting lessons have been learned about this from studies conducted with institutionalized children. In some cases children received excellent physical and medical care. They were fed regularly, received clothing changes, and remained warm and dry. But often the institutional staff did not have time to nurture each child. In one study, Dr. Rene Spitz found only one fourth of these children between ages two and four could walk unassisted. He also found problems in the children's abilities to dress themselves and speak at their age level. Spitz described the children as physically, socially, and emotionally retarded.

The importance of attention, love, and a balanced family environment cannot be overemphasized. Children reared in this type of setting will have tremendous advantages over those who aren't. A balanced environment not only allows your child to prosper physically, but also is a necessity for high self-esteem and self-achievement. It's vital in the pathway to later independence. Studies have found that children ignored by their parents (or primary caretakers) have lower IQ scores, show more aggressiveness, exhibit less initiative, and interact with less warmth. In later years these children fail to have a strong sense of identity. The sense of "self" appears to be somehow lost, or absorbed by a group, or another person. Unfortunately, these same traits may be carried into adulthood.

Mrs. Sims's manner was apologetic as she joined the group. It was her first visit. She unobtrusively found an open seat, carefully avoiding eye contact with anyone. Her deep auburn hair framed a frozen, almost expressionless face. She riveted her gaze on a spot in the carpet as if in a trance, scarcely moving and never changing expression.

She was a stately looking woman, but projected some indescribably etched pain from her otherwise concrete features. Group members began introducing themselves as she sat, failing to acknowledge their comments. I suddenly realized that she was the only one who had not spoken.

"We're all here for a reason," I intervened. "I guess we're all pretty much alike. We're fallible human beings. We're still growing and everyone of us has experienced pain. I think we also have the capacity to help each other by sharing some of that. Mrs. Sims, you're our newest member. I'd like for you to explain to the group why you're here."

A shattering silence followed for what must have been two or three minutes. She continued to stare fixedly at the floor. Several group members began to shift their positions uncomfortably from side to side. Others cleared their throats. Someone coughed. I anxiously wiggled my toes in secret harmony and began to feel a bit inadequate against the silence. I was aware most of the group members were probably more uncomfortable than I. Americans don't seem at ease without noise, I thought to myself. I had learned from the Mountangard tribesmen of Vietnam to make friends with silence. But in this setting I felt responsible. My mind began to wander.

"I—I—I've never done this before," she struggled to say. "I'm not really good at this kind of thing." She looked up from the carpet. I noticed her eyes for the first time. They seemed the same auburn color as her hair and not as tense as before.

"I just went through a divorce less than a year ago. I was married for twenty years. I have two children in college and one getting ready to leave home soon. I have never been *anybody*," she stated emphatically.

"I married Ted before I graduated from high school. He's quite a bit older and had everything going for him. He was very wealthy. I've always been Mrs. Ted Sims, or Buffy's mother, or Jim's daughter. But I've never been *anybody*.

"All I ever wanted was some attention. I never got it at home. Mom worked in Daddy's business. They both drank all the time. I never got anything from them. So I married Ted. I figured he was older. He'd take care of me. And he did. Oh, did he ever! Drinking, affairs, lies. But what should I have expected?

"All my life, all I've ever wanted was to be loved. To be loved, and to be somebody. I guess that's why I'm here."

She looked up and made eye contact with me for the first time. "Is that asking too much, Dr. Baucom? Is it asking so much to be loved just once in your lifetime?"

The tears she was holding back erupted. She shook rhythmically as she sobbed. Two ladies left their seats and moved toward her. One carried tissues and offered them to Mrs. Sims. They wrapped their arms around her, and all three began to cry together.

I sat and silently watched, unable to respond. The three together were the only answer needed.

Mrs. Sims is a good example of an adult who has lived in an emotional void most of her life. The result was her sadness and lack of identity. Nurturing attention needs to occur not only during early infancy but throughout life. From neonatal intensive care units all the way to nursing homes, we find the results of its absence. It happens in all age ranges. And it can happen to our own children. The preventive measure is to find the appropriate balance of attention and nurture for your children. To accomplish this requires understanding several components, the most important of which is attitude.

ATTITUDE

Many attitudes toward children aren't very encouraging. Some religious leaders condemn teenagers as "uncivilized and depraved" and even today suggest beating the demons out of them. But there is no research, experience, or even theory to support their perspective. The authority they repeatedly cite doesn't seem to agree with them. The Bible gives many examples of Christ exhibiting love and nurturing attention toward children. He brought children to his side and took them on his lap. On several occasions he raised children from the dead and even reminded the parents of one child to feed the child before celebrating. This showed an incredible sensitivity to children's needs.

He manifested the attitude of "loving the sinner, but not necessarily the sin." Various examples emphasize the importance Christ placed on the person above and beyond any problem the person might be experiencing. At one point, after restoring sight to a man, he used the occasion to correct the false belief that the handicap was a result of sin, either by him or his parents. Another time he cast out demons who possessed a man living like an animal among tombs. Rather than being disgusted by him or rebuking him, Jesus sent the man on a mission to his own people. He was to report the mercy and goodness shown to him. Even Judas, the disciple who betrayed Christ, was not rebuked for his dishonorable behavior.

Christ did not condone the behavior in these examples. But he also did not condemn the "misbehaver." His attitude was one of nurturing attention with no implied criticism. This is an excellent attitude for parents to model. You can love and accept the "misbehaver," without condoning the "behavior." Your love and acceptance can never be in doubt. Your child needs constant reassurance of your compassion, regardless of the circumstances, and regardless of his behavior.

Attitude is the basic fundamental element for structuring

an appropriate balance of attention for your child. Upon this basis, other qualities are added. The first of these is a strong parent-child bond.

BONDING

Imagine a grown man, strutting and dancing, with a mature female crane. He stands on one foot, flaps his arms like two pretend wings, and thrusts his neck back and forth. He chases the crane in a circle several times, and then she runs away. The crane, at an early age, had apparently imprinted, and later, bonded with this man. It was necessary for him to go through this ritual so that the crane would begin her nesting.

Konrad Lorenz was one of the first scientists to study the phenomenon of imprinting. He applied this term to the critical period when environmental influences have their greatest effect on infant development. Lorenz has shown that very young geese, ducks, and some other birds will automatically identify with or imprint on the first moving object they see. This could be another duck, a human, or even an inanimate object, such as a ball or lawn mover. With geese, once this imprinting occurs, it is permanent. As in the above case, some researchers found mature geese who imprinted on humans as goslings have difficulty in later sexual development relating to birds of their own species.

This behavior has been noticed in other animals as well. As a teenager I lived on a farm in western North Carolina. Each year my step-father gave a lamb to his niece. She raised the lamb with her dogs and fed it from a bottle. The lamb would begin acting like a dog and appeared to have difficulty with other sheep! It even slept in the dog house, snuggled next to its favorite hound.

A fellow student in college raised and sold poodles. Somehow he had been given a five-week-old Saint Bernard. The Saint Bernard was naturally raised alongside the small poodles. The pup seemed to adopt one of the poodles as a foster mother. Later, it was hilarious to watch a two-hundred-pound Saint Bernard jump nervously up and down and yap like a poodle! He apparently had imprinted the characteristics of a hyperactive poodle.

Some researchers believe there is a similar phenomenon that occurs in human infants. There are different suggestions as to when and how often these critical bonding periods occur. Some writers suggest one such period is within the first ninety minutes of birth. Others have theorized there are several different sensitive periods. Certainly, these times would revolve around emotionally intense moments when sensory awareness is heightened, such as birth, breast-feeding, and the first few days of life. This would imply it's best for parents to be in the proximity of their young children during these moments of heightened sensory intensity.

Apparently, imprinting can be activated by close physical contact. Holding, caressing, and rocking are examples of triggers to elicit imprinting. Smiling, calling, and approaching the infant could also assist in this process. During Bennie's pregnancies I spoke to the children, intrauterine, on a nightly basis. I'm sure if anyone would have observed this process as I spoke to my wife's obviously pregnant stomach, they would have been very curious. After Chip's birth, he greeted the world with a nonstop wail. Finally, when I got my chance to hold him, I began to speak. He instantly quieted and turned his head. While still safe within the womb, he had apparently imprinted on his dad's voice.

Some authorities use the terms bonding and imprinting interchangeably. Imprinting is a phenomenon that certainly occurs in some animals and may occur in humans. Frankly, the research has been disputed and is not universally accepted. This is especially true when researchers attempt to attach a definite time limit to the concept of a critical period. Those who suggest it only occurs during the first ninety minutes after the child's birth have received the most disagreement. However, the final verdict is not in. The term bonding is used to define the entire process of forming the intense parent-child, grandparent-child, or primary caretaker-child bond. For the purpose of this book, it can include the imprinting period, but it involves more.

Bonding is aided by close physical contact. But whereas imprinting classically occurs with only one object, bonding can occur with several. Bonding is also a clear case of when "quantity time" is more important than "quality time." The more time you devote to your child, the more bonding can occur. One controlled study found children who had bonded well with their primary caretakers had significantly higher IQ scores by age five and were more advanced in language and verbal skills.

Bonding usually requires time spent with the child in eye contact, holding, hugging, playing, moving, watching, listening, rocking, swinging, and other such activity. It requires patience. And although the concept is abstract, once bonding is cemented, the adult is aware of it. Bonding apparently activates certain potentials in children. The process of bonding is one of extreme intensity. This period is followed by what will be referred to as attachment and identity formation.

ATTACHMENT

Attachment begins in early infancy and continues throughout the growth process. Technically, attachment occurs when a feeling of warmth and permanence toward another is formed. This can be a parent, sibling, or some other individual. However, attachment can also occur toward an object, such as a blanket, article of clothing, or even a car. A child's attachment will initially be toward the primary caretaker, usually the mother or mother substitute. Within only a brief period, however, it is clear that attachment can occur with others.

Although time certainly influences attachment, it is not absolutely necessary that the infant have constant exposure to the attachment object. One study found mothers who are away most of the day can have as strong an attachment as mothers who are home. The quality of the relationship may provide sufficient stimulus for the attachment to continue. Often, following attachment to family members, a child will form object attachment.

Keppy, my eldest son, owned his first football jersey before he was even born. I stocked him up with all sizes and colors. He still has enough to last through early adulthood. Naturally, he prefers the Chicago Bears; so we get along real well! Somehow, though, much to my embarrassment, he became the proud owner of a Washington Redskins jersey. Keppy started wearing it constantly. It didn't matter that it hadn't been washed in a couple of weeks. He wanted to wear it! It didn't matter that the Redskins were losing. And most of all, it didn't matter that his dad was a Bears fan. Keppy liked the Redskins jersey! We began trying to sneak it off of him after he went to sleep and sneak on a Bears jersey. That didn't work! We were becoming a neighborhood embarrassment!

Finally, we parents of this "wayward" child decided to assert ourselves. Enough insult is enough! He had to take off that jersey. And he did. But we had underestimated the power of attachment.

He went out the door with a beautiful Bears jersey on his back. In his right hand, dragging on the floor like Linus's security blanket, was his attachment object. My son had bonded with a Redskin football jersey! And no amount of nurture could break it away!

IDENTITY

Nurture grows very important during the entire phase of identity formation. The power of nurturing attention cannot be overstated. It can even overcome the lack of early childhood deprivation. The story of Isabelle in chapter 1 is a good example. The first six years of her life she was extremely deprived. Yet with the stimulation of her mother and a team of researchers from Ohio State University, she was able to make up the difference. Incidentally, Isabelle later completed high school, married, and had children of her own.

Another example comes from a well-documented case involving twin boys. Psychologist Jarmila Koluchova worked with the twins, who suffered extreme abuse and deprivation up to age seven. They had been physically beaten, locked up for long periods of time in a cellar, and not fed properly. The twins even suffered from lack of fresh air, sunlight, and exposure.

At age seven, they were placed in a very stimulating foster home. The boys were initially labeled severely mentally retarded and given little hope for the future. But, in the new environment they quickly progressed. By fourteen years of age, the twins had IQs of over 100 (average to above average). Their social skills had improved, and they had formed friends. There was none of the near animal-like timidity as before. In all aspects the young boys were considered normal. Koluchova concluded that "gross damage, previously considered to be irreversible, can be remedied." In this case the remedy was nurturing attention provided by loving foster parents.

The process of identity occurs as children ultimately discover "who they are" and the various aspects of their uniqueness. At the same time that identity formation is occuring, so is detachment. The process of detachment involves outwardly separating from one's parents.

INDEPENDENCE

Your child's first day at school introduces the building block of beginning detachment and independence. Although traumatic, this is both necessary and healthy. At this point parental influence weakens and peer ties are strengthened. The process continues throughout the teen years. The late teenager needs to grow increasingly independent. Parents who do not encourage this process are literally stunting the emotional growth of their children.

The story of Bob at the beginning of this chapter is an

equally sad and true example. At age twenty-three his parents not only prevented him from getting a job but also refused his participation in housekeeping activities. I later discovered that when he tried to do his own laundry or get a part-time job, they belittled his efforts, convinced him he was incompetent, and did it for him. When Bob attempted to break away from them, he was prevented from doing so. Bob became so dependent on his parents, he couldn't keep a job. In fact, he had few employable skills. There was consequently, in his mind, no way to support himself financially. All he could see was a trap that blocked his attempts to detach from his parents and to establish independence.

I am also convinced that Bob's parents had the absolute best of intentions. But this is another testimony to the fact that good intentions are never enough. As parents, we want the best for our children. When watching them struggle we often want to interfere and help. As parents, out of love, we often prevent our children from experiencing the natural consequences of their behavior. In doing so, we unknowingly create long term problems in return for short term answers.

Detachment and independence are both vital. The process is gradual and must be encouraged by parents. The alternative is the enmeshment that occurs from chronic parental overinvolvement when personal boundaries are not respected and individual identity development is actually obstructed.

ENMESHMENT

In many ways it was a typical family session. The parents sat on the couch together. Deep lines cut into their leathery faces. Their voices expressed concern about "the boy."

I wondered how he felt about being constantly referred to in the third person. They didn't call him by his first name, Jack, or a more endearing "our son." It was always "the boy."

The parents weren't hostile. In fact, their presentation was filled with love. They were very endearing parents. I could tell they loved the boy. He could tell, too. As they spoke, he grinned somewhat sheepishly. When they began discussing his drug use, he seemed embarrassed but also slightly amused.

The boy was as thin as an anorectic teenager. His pale skin had a soft, ivory tint. His long, matted hair hid his ears and hung almost to midback. His skinny fingers were calloused from what looked like cigarette burns. Decked out in jeans and a jacket, he was dressed as a typical adolescent. Several times he pulled back his jacket so I wouldn't miss the alligator on his knit shirt. He seemed somewhat detached from the session, like he was not really a participant. The discussion was "about him," not "with him." And no matter how actively I tried, I failed to get him involved.

The boy had been in jail more times than his aging parents could count. Each time, they bailed him out and paid his legal fees. He had been doing drugs since his early teenage years. Hospitalizations and drug treatment programs had not helped. Each time he called his parents to take him out they did. His mother still washed, ironed, cooked, and cleaned while the boy listened to music and slept. Of course he stayed out late at night while they slept. And he slept while they worked to support him. Since he didn't work, they gave him a regular allowance.

The boy was not dumb. His IQ was tested to be 140. Naturally, his academic level did not demonstrate his IQ. He dropped out in the eleventh grade, but he was still bright. He had held several jobs. At one point he was an extremely successful salesman of business machines.

Of course that was when he was married. His wife left him after two years. She couldn't put up with his extreme dependence; so he had been in and out of his parents' house since then. They encouraged him to "just stay there permanently."

Their primary fear was the future. Who would take care of him when they died? The parents were in their 70s.

The boy was forty-two years old.

Although Andy drooled, limped, and couldn't speak, there was no record of serious impairment in spite of being "trashed" as an infant. Over a period of weeks, I requested X rays, brain scans, and other neurological tests. No damage was found. Sometime during those weeks I became very attached to Andy and took more than a professional interest in his case.

On a whim, I asked Tony and Jane to begin visiting Andy. I had known them for some time and realized they had love to give to a child. They were in their late thirties at the time and had lost their only child in an automobile accident several years earlier. Since then they had been unable to adopt another child. Their initial visits with Andy went well, and they soon became regulars during visitation. From then on I became their "coach" with Andy.

Andy had never lived with a family. Institutionalization was the only life he had known. To my knowledge, he had never sat at a family supper table, played with uninstitutionalized children, or celebrated a holiday the way others do. All he had ever been exposed to were staff members of the hospital and the children with various handicaps, most of whom also had some degree of retardation.

I wondered if he had adapted and learned to be "normal" in this environment. To be normal in this facility would be to limp, drool, or groan instead of speak. My questions became a nuisance with administrators. But nobody could disagree with the difference the Cox family had made with Andy. He learned to recognize them and was even attempting to sound out their names. Later, I noticed he neither limped nor drooled when around them. But as soon as they left, he resumed his old behavior.

Within a few months the Cox family was allowed to keep Andy at their home on weekends and holidays. They decorated a bedroom for him and took him to movies and Sunday school. They had a birthday party for him and even taught him to ride a bicycle with training wheels. A few months later the training wheels came off. Andy was soon speaking several words, kicking a soccer ball, and learning to play with younger children. He began to identify people by name and to actually call names aloud. Still, each time we returned to the hospital, he regressed.

From the time I first invited the Cox family to visit Andy, it was only six months before they initially asked about adopting him. They were convinced he was a normal child. So was I. Institutional authorities, however, were not. It took over eighteen months, several thousand dollars in legal fees, and hundreds of hours of work to change their minds. But the Coxs eventually adopted Andy. I resigned my position at the hospital a few days later. I was viewed as a troublemaker by this time.

And now Andy was graduating from high school, only a few years behind schedule. My belief in the power of nurture had been reinforced. This was a modern miracle. It was a tearful occasion. I coughed and cleared my throat. Several people looked at me uncomfortably. I blew my nose. They stared angrily. When Andy's name was called, I shouted out loud. They asked me to please be quiet.

I blew my nose again.

I guess I'm still a troublemaker.

IMPROVING YOUR PARENTING ART

STRUCTURING A POSITIVE ENVIRONMENT

1. What were the negative and positive elements of your own childhood? Are any of these elements being repeated today in your family? How can you change the negative elements?

2. What would you change about your childhood environment? Leave the same? Would you choose different models for yourself?

3. Who do you see yourself modeling after as a parent? Are you satisfied with this image? As a parent, what characteristics are your strongest? Your weakest as related to structuring a positive environment?

4. What do your children think about their environment? Are they behaving according to your expectations? If not, review again your modeling as well as your verbal instructions. Do you reward the positive behavior or do you find yourself giving greatest attention to the negative behavior?

5. How do you rate yourself as a parent? Are you underinvolved? Overinvolved? Balanced? Are you willing to grant your children their independence?

PARENTING EXERCISES

Have a family meeting. With all members present, discuss what can be done to improve the home environment. Get comments from each family member. Also question whether or not family members are getting enough individual attention. Have each participant state what they need specifically to feel more loved at home. Decide on a thirty-day-trial plan for meeting these needs. In a highly visible spot, post the written needs and the action plan to meet them. After thirty days, have another family meeting to discuss feelings about the experiment.

Greet one another with a holy kiss.
                              —*2 Corinthians 13:12*

Greet one another with a kiss of love.
                              —*1 Peter 5:14*

This is the greatest sin of you and me and all of us.
To have more power than love; more knowledge
than understanding; more information about the
earth than the people who live on it; more skill to
fly to far off places than to stop a moment and
look within our own heart. For freedom is a
dreadful word unless it goes hand in hand with
responsibility. And democracy is going to disappear from the face of the earth unless the minds of
men grow mature.

                              —*Lillian Smith*

6

Touch Your Child

TWO A.M. silence. The full moon kissed night's quiet darkness, and a nocturnal cricket symphony soothed me into a deep sleep. The past week had been long and demanding, and I sought solace in my dreams. I floated to the cricket concert being performed outside my open window. In the warm April evening, I found peace. Rest.

My trance shattered by the piercing ring of a new phone, I groped through the quicksand of sleep and pulled the telephone to my ear. I began to speak while it still rang. "Silly thing has a switch," I thought to myself. As I searched for the way to turn it on, the phone continued to shriek. I grumbled under my breath.

"Hello," I said into the earpiece. I turned it right side up and spoke again. "Uh, hello?"

"John?" the heavily accented voice asked.

"Huh?" I answered. After all, it was two o'clock in the morning; the caller couldn't expect anything too clever.

The caller tried again to communicate with me. "Hello, my name is Angelina Grego," she said in Italian-spiced

English. "I am old and don't have no money to pay you. But my priest told me to call you, anyway. He thinks I need to see a shrink."

I don't think of myself as a shrink. Actually, I think of myself as a person who helps people expand their minds. I don't like the negative connotation shrink has, which was heightened by the woman's sarcastic emphasis.

After pausing, I responded. "Well, I'm not much of a shrink, and I really can't tell you if you need to see one or not. It would help if you could give me some idea of why your priest said that."

"It's bad," she interrupted. "It's real bad. I just feel awful. Sometimes I think I can't go on. I just—just feel awful—terrible." The words were garbled by her mournful crying.

My first instinct is always to prevent people from crying and to attempt to fix things. Through the years I've learned, however, that many times it's just as important to let people get the tears out. I remained silent while Mrs. Grego continued to weep. Finally, after a few moments of silence, I began to speak.

"Mrs. Grego, I can tell you're real sad. It's probably best if I see you at my office in the morning. We can work you in, I'm sure."

"I don't even know that it's worth it," she pouted. "I'm sure all your other patients are more important than me. Besides, you can't bring back the dead, can you?"

This was my first indication of what was troubling her. "No, Ma'am. You're right," I assured her. "I definitely can't. It sounds like you lost someone very close to you, though. I'm sure it hurts. Sometimes talking about the loss of someone close to you helps." I tried to comfort her, but I was interrupted by her sudden scream.

"No, you don't understand!" she screeched. "She wasn't someone. She was my only friend. Marla was the only one in the world who loved me. She was my parakeet. And now you probably think I'm crazy, just like Father Tom does."

"*Your parakeet?*" *I was startled. I wondered if the call was a set-up. Who would be playing a joke on me? But I tried to stay serious, just in case the woman was for real. "Your parakeet has died? Uh, what a loss." I tried to sound sincere. "Listen, Mrs. Grego, I think it probably is a good idea that you make an appointment so we can talk about this in person."*

The next day we met. She had indeed been serious. And she was very depressed.

HUGGING

One of the first true marriage and family counselors in the United States was my former professor and mentor, the late Dr. Clinton Phillips. Clint, as he was affectionately known, was also one of the most creative people I have ever met. He directly or indirectly had a major positive influence on thousands of professional marriage and family therapists who have in turn helped hundreds of thousands of others.

I recall Clint once coming into the classroom and unexpectedly suggesting we should each seek out a minimum of thirty-one hugs daily. I don't remember the particular magic associated with the number thirty-one. It seems he cited a UCLA study that had discovered thirty-one hugs provided sufficient neurological and sensory stimulation for optimal health. A few weeks later I noticed a license plate on campus that read "31 HUGS." Eventually, a ritual developed in which several of us began seeking out that precise number. Although we pursued it in a humorous way, we actually began to look forward to our daily portion. If for some reason we didn't meet the quota, life actually seemed to be less rewarding.

Retrospectively, it's doubtful a hug had much to do with how our days went. But the physical contact and touch probably did. Touch is extremely important for adults and absolutely necessary for the proper development of our children. There are actual documented cases of adults and children dying due to a lack of touch. To understand the importance of touch, we must first understand the skin.

Skin has been described as the largest and most ignored organ of the body. The average human body has eighteen square feet of skin, studded with approximately five million microscopic nerve endings. There are specific nerve endings for different sensations such as pain, heat, and cold. When touched, the appropriate nerve endings are activated. They then relay their sensory messages through the spinal cord to the brain. Research indicates that without sufficient stimulation of these nerve endings an infant can be doomed to premature death. The entire process of sensory and skin stimulation occurs through touch.

I have been a lover and owner of a variety of animals. For several years during my adolescence, I lived and worked on a farm. We had sheep, pigs, chickens, horses, dogs, cats, and an occasional visiting skunk. On one occasion a small bear even tried to join our family! That was stimulating for everyone, especially our collie who hid underneath the back porch. I have vivid memories of the entire period and warmly recall the frequency with which all of these animals used the sense of touch to communicate. In fact, without exception, the animals nudged and licked their young immediately after giving birth. This touch appeared to stimulate the newborn into active life itself.

Touch and other forms of physical contact may be the food required by skin, as well as the emotions, to sustain growth. The sense of touch may be the most powerful communication tool available. It is one of the first communication channels that is present at birth and remains available throughout life. Hugging, cuddling, and caressing are all not only effective tools of expression but also possible avenues to healing. Effective as touch is, we are more often than not intimidated by it. Modern society is not one that values touch. In fact, Western culture is somewhat suspicious of anyone who is comfortable with it. The subtle discouragement and disapproval of such contact is an unfortunate denial of a very special part of being human. And this denial is more often found in our own modern culture than any other.

Americans use handshakes as a way to exchange greetings. A handshake can be vigorous or superficial. Either way it's quite sterile when compared with social greetings exchanged by other cultures. A friend visited me several years ago from South Africa. He was not totally familiar with American customs and at times his affection resulted in some suspicious glances. While shopping with me in a mall, he interlocked his arm in mine and left it there. I am not used to walking arm in arm with other men, but I didn't wish to offend my colleague. In his culture this was apparently accepted social behavior.

On another occasion, many years earlier in Vietnam, I was kissed on the mouth by a Mountangard tribesman as a gesture of appreciation after I carried him, unconscious and wounded, for fifteen miles through the jungle. In his opinion, I had saved his life. Later, during a ceremony, I was thanked by his entire family, including his brothers, who also felt obligated to hug and kiss me. In the United States, such an expression would have been discouraged and disapproved.

I was initially uncomfortable with the Mountangard custom as well as with my South African friend's behavior. In that way, I'm probably representative of American culture, but I'm not convinced that our aloofness is entirely healthy. Many other cultures are much more demonstrative in fulfilling their need for touch. We only need to visit another country or view the nightly news to become aware that Americans are in a minority. When Russians greet each other, they embrace. So do most Orientals, Europeans, and Latin Americans. This exchange of greetings is usually brief. Two people grasp each other by the shoulders and kiss or brush lightly on each other's cheek. Often times a verbal exchange occurs. Greeks often say Se Agapo, which means "I love you," as they embrace. The Italians hug when saying hello and good-bye.

Westerners appear less willing to experiment with similar

contact. In fact, Americans usually need more space or individual distance than all other modern cultures. There are reports of Americans traveling abroad, especially in the Mideast, who found the residents of those countries standing uncomfortably close. Yet, the social distance required by Americans is interpreted in these cultures as being offensively distant, even rude. Our lack of comfort probably is merely a cultural learning that touch is objectionable in some way. Still, research demonstrates the need and even craving for touch is undeniable.

LACK OF TOUCH

It would be immoral to conduct controlled laboratory experiments on humans to scientifically investigate the effects of touch deprivation. Without research, however, there is no way to understand the social, emotional, and even physiological problems resulting from lack of physical contact. Most researchers have attempted to look at results in noncontrolled settings. Other researchers have conducted controlled laboratory experiments with animals.

The most widely reported of these researchers has been Harry Harlow and his colleagues at the University of Wisconsin. Harlow's research was completed primarily with primates such as rhesus monkeys. While we cannot unequivocally apply all of Harlow's work directly to humans, there are certainly many applications. The results of his work have fascinated readers for the past twenty-five years.

Among other things, Harlow experimented with raising monkeys in varying degrees of isolation. In one study some of the monkeys received no social contact whatever. Others received contact with wire models of grown monkeys or terry cloth models of other monkeys. Some in the experiments could make contact with other monkeys but only through wires separating their cages. Generally, the more isolation a monkey experienced, the more bizarre his behavior appeared. Isolated monkeys were increasingly fearful and hostile. They appeared generally apathetic and depressed. As adults, they were unable to relate to or mate with other monkeys. If the females who were raised in isolation became pregnant by artificial insemination, they were rejecting, abusive, and often homicidal as mothers.

Dr. James Prescott from the National Institute of Child Health and Human Development thinks this aspect of Harlow's work is directly applicable to human families. In one study of abused children it was found that the abusive parents were invariably deprived of physical contact themselves during childhood. Dr. Prescott states that deprivation of touch during the formative years of life is a major contributing factor to later violence. This finding is identical to the results of Harlow's research with monkeys. Prescott continues to suggest that touch deprivation may also cause depression, autism, and even drug abuse.

The young monkeys in Harlow's studies seemed to be more interested in physical contact than food. In one set of experiments a terry cloth model of an adult monkey was placed in the cage. Alongside was a wire model adult monkey who was holding a bottle. The young monkey would cling to the terry cloth "mother," rejecting the wire model except during times of feeding. Research with other animals has revealed similar results. Some have demonstrated serious brain and neurological damage resulting from isolation and lack of touch.

Other studies indicated that increased contact and stimulation can lead to a well-adapted and energetic infant, with a more fully-developed brain and neurological system. As this study illustrated, increased physical contact apparently can help reverse damage caused by previous touch deprivation. This finding is well supported by other studies.

One researcher found that prematurely born infants gained weight faster when placed on lamb's wool rather than on ordinary cotton sheets. Apparently, physical contact with the lamb's wool stimulates growth. In a similar study, premature infants were given an added fifteen-minute period of massage and stroking daily. The effects of the touching were dramatic. The stroked infants gained more weight than those not stroked.

Austrian scientist Rene Spitz visited orphanages and foundling homes to investigate the effect these institutions had on children. His curiosity was aroused because of the crowded conditions of these facilities during World War II, as well as their history of results with children. As an historical example, records of the Dublin Foundling Home indicated that between 1775 and 1800 only 45 out of 10,272 children admitted, survived their stay there. In 1915, ninety percent of infants in Baltimore orphanages died within a year of admission. These numbers seem startling, yet their accuracy is unquestioned. Further investigation by Spitz and others revealed similar results around the world.

Recent studies found optimistic mortality results but equally discouraging factors in other ways. As an example, due to staff shortages at a foundling home in Beirut, Lebanon, infants were not receiving enough physical contact. In fact, the children were restricted from sufficient physical movement. Most of their time was spent in cribs and playpens. When tested, the children were discovered to have an average IQ of 53. Those who were adopted within the first two years of life improved rapidly and by age four had an IQ of 100, which is considered average. Those adopted at a later age did have an IQ increase but not as substantial as those adopted earlier. Spitz declared the difference to be due to lack of adequate physical contact and interaction. Those children adopted earlier received more intense physical contact at a younger age.

Researchers have demonstrated time and time again that increased levels of touching and other sensory contact can improve the health and functioning of institutionalized children. As an example, Spitz enlisted grandmother-aged women to simply rock, cuddle, and interact with infants in one understaffed and overcrowded orphanage. Mortality rates improved as well as general levels of health, intelligence, and social skills. Cuddling, rocking, swinging, and gentle physical play can serve as growth stimulants to children of all ages.

HEALING TOUCH

Recently, researchers have begun to recognize touch as a painkiller. Some describe it as having an antidepressant effect. Therapeutic massage has long been recognized as having rehabilitative value in people who have experienced muscular and orthopedic damage. In American society, touching is often seen as a way of comforting someone who is sick, impaired, or bereaved. A mother gently rubbing the stomach of her sick child is an example. A passing motorist observes an accident along the roadside. The conscious but injured driver is grimacing. A passenger in the car holds his hand comfortingly. Another man grieves the death of his elderly parent. His brother-in-law holds him as the man sobs. Touch is seen in all these cases as healing in nature.

In one study, physical contact led to reduced levels of anxiety in patients hospitalized for cardiovascular disorders. Another found absence of physical contact associated with depression. Those who were more depressed expressed a greater need for physical contact than those not depressed. In an educational setting hugging was successfully used as a way to motivate inattentive fifth graders. The students became more cooperative and reported greater enjoyment of class. A West German insurance company claims men who touch and kiss their wives make thirty percent more income over a life span than those who don't. Another study found hugging increases hemoglobin in the blood. And the research continues.

Unfortunately, as simple and effective as physical contact is, Americans are not touchers. American parents are less likely to make physical contact with their children than are parents from other cultures. Prolific researcher and psychologist Dr. Sidney Jourard, from the University of Florida, provides a dramatic example of this. During social conversation in restaurants, he counted Puerto Ricans touching each other 180 times per hour. In the same setting, French people made physical contact 110 times per hour. Dr. Jourard made the same series of observations in the United States. The result was startling—two contacts per hour. That is a graphic and discouraging statistic.

In stressful or critical periods of life, touch is often an antidote to pain. It would seem we could use the magic touch for preventive as well as curative measures. Several years ago a television special discussed the significance of touch. A study was cited which investigated social factors influencing recovery from heart attack. The social factors questioned included such issues as marital status, presence of extended family, church attendance, and type of neighborhood.

The purpose of the study was to isolate the social factors that would predispose a person to more quickly recover from heart attack. Obviously, this would be of value, not only to researchers, but also to recovering victims. The study was conducted with as much scientific rigor as possible. Appropriate controls were used. Initial results seemed to arouse more questions than answers. The social factor with the most significant impact was pet ownership! That factor proved to be more positively correlated to recovery from heart attack than any other, including marital status. The issue was blurred by this result.

After further analysis of the data, the significance of pet ownership became more clear. Researchers already realized men suffer from heart failure more often than women. In our society it is more acceptable for women to touch others than it is for men. There are apparently certain social stigmas preventing men from touching to any great degree. However, there is little stigma attached to men touching pets. In fact, there is even some unspoken sanction to encourage man and dog contact. Rubbing a pet also can be done almost unconsciously. Perhaps there is greater significance than once thought to the adage that "a dog is man's best friend." The final implication of this study was that men who own pets are more likely to experience stimulating touch. However, touch was primarily from their dogs or cats rather than people.

This study concludes that touch is so therapeutic it could help people recover from heart attack. Touch can probably even act to prevent such a malady. It's interesting to consider the implication of such a study. We are forced to consider whether in some parts of American culture it is more acceptable for a man to touch his Doberman than another person. If true, it's an interesting comment on the power of touch and a disturbing comment about social stigma.

Nevertheless, the results of all these studies indicate touch is a healthy, vital process, and of major importance to your children. Your child needs touch. It is vital for health and necessary for life itself.

HOLY KISS

When away from home on weekends I enjoy visiting new churches. It's a habit I began as a child. My parents enjoyed it, and I began doing it with them. Several years ago I visited a church in Southern California. When leaving I noticed a young bearded man standing at the door laughing. He was hugging people as they left. He appeared to be causing a major, but humorous disruption, as people teased him.

"Don't let him scare you," an elderly woman assured me. "He's our holy kisser."

"He's what?" I asked while laughing.

"He's our holy kisser," she giggled excitedly. "He decided he was going to follow Paul's advice, and so he made himself the official holy kisser. Ain't it wonderful? It's the only hug I get all week. He don't smell bad either!"

I laughed again as the woman worked her way up to the young man. They wrapped their arms around each other and exchanged a vigorous hug. She patted him on the back as he lifted her up off the ground. The embrace lasted a few seconds, and then it was my turn!

"Lift me up, too!" I joked. He laughed, gave me a quick hug, and then shook my hand.

"I'm Charlie, the holy kisser," he explained.

"Glad to meet you, Charlie," I responded. "I'm John and I'm just visiting." After exchanging greetings, Charlie explained that he had decided to become the "holy kisser" after reading the apostle Paul's writings.

"You know, Peter suggested the same thing," he assured me.

"Sounds good to me. I think it's a great tradition," I responded.

"And it's biblical too!" Charlie added.

The apostle Paul suggested to the Romans, Corinthians, and Thessalonians to "greet each other with a holy kiss." Peter suggested a similar greeting to all Christians. Apparently, Charlie decided that was a modern-day mission he could fulfill. Although such behavior is counterculture today, it was common when Paul wrote his letters. There is also evidence that Christ used physical contact. On many occasions he touched people to heal them. There are other cases of people being healed from merely touching Christ's clothing.

In his interpretation of creation, Michelangelo shows God and man almost touching, their barely separated fingers implying communication and caring. King David also spoke of a child resting against his mother as quieting to the soul. Most of us are familiar with the plea to "kiss it and make it better." Somehow the magic works! It gets better.

One of my grandmother's favorite rituals was what she called "nussing." This involved holding us in her lap and rocking back and forth, hugging. Many nights there would be a line of children waiting on the front porch. As she sat in her wooden rocker, they would ask, "Nuss me, Granny." She would give each his turn. Granny's touch communicated far more than mere words ever could. I was the luckiest of all the children in our neighborhood. I got to live with her! And in her later years, we traded places. I got to "nuss" her! There have been many times in therapy when I have wanted to tell parents to "just nuss him" and it will be okay. As I observed a family in my office several years ago I thought of Granny again.

LEARNING TO TOUCH

Apathy masked whatever horror was boiling inside them all. The parents were tired, but quietly angry and stoic. They had been to dozens of experts and had no idea where to turn next. The entire family exuded a sense of desperation. Of immediate concern was their fourteen-year-old son, Terry. On several occasions they discovered him dressed in his older sister's clothing. Five separate times he had serious conversations with both parents about becoming a girl. Once he asked a school teacher if he could get an operation to make him a girl. Apparently, he had heard something on television about such a procedure. His parents were overwhelmed with confusion.

During the interview with Terry, several issues became clear. He was extremely uncomfortable with physical and aggressive play. Growing up with three sisters had not presented opportunities for wrestling or playing ball. His father was a successful businessman who was gone most of the time. And from Terry's perspective it appeared that his father favored the girls. They seemed to get more attention. Everyone in the family admitted that the daughters received more physical contact from their father.

"Do you hug Terry very often?" I asked the father during a session.

"No, not a lot." He seemed to be thinking aloud. "I really don't."

"How about physical stuff?" I wondered. "Wrestling, football, chasing?"

"No. I won't do that." He responded somewhat indignantly. "I really am not comfortable with that kind of activity. My father didn't do that with me, and I just don't think it's proper."

I paused, and the father crossed his arms and glared in my direction. The mother cradled her forehead with both hands. Her gaze remained fixed on the floor.

"You see, Dr. Baucom, this is part of the problem. Jim is so upset about Terry that he won't go near him. He simply will not have anything to do with him. I feel like I have to make up for that attention. Terry is scared of his dad and I think, quite honestly, Jim is scared of Terry. Jim is so intimidated by all of this, he won't even talk to anyone at home. So we had to come all the way down here."

After a brief silence I turned. "Jim, tell me about you and your dad. What was growing up like for you?"

As Jim spoke, the pieces of the puzzle began to fall together. Jim had never been close to his father. Though his parents were both alive, Jim had not seen them in over nine years. He had last spoken to them on the telephone six years earlier. His wife and the children were forbidden to contact or return telephone calls to Jim's family. During his childhood, Jim's father was an active alcoholic. Most of the time Jim was either abused or ignored. There seemed to be no middle ground and certainly no intimacy. To protect himself, Jim had subconsciously withdrawn from his father.

As a result, there had been no role model for Jim to learn appropriate forms of physical touch or physical play with other males. As a father of three daughters, this was no problem. He had no difficulty as a child relating to his mother, aunts, or sisters. So Jim felt comfortable dealing with his own daughters, both emotionally and physically. When Terry was born, however, the problems from Jim's past surfaced. In fact, shortly after Terry's birth, Jim withdrew from his own parents. Shortly thereafter, his career changed, and he began traveling more frequently. Upon returning home from the frequent trips, Jim directed his attention to the girls who, due to their ages, were capable of responding more openly. Jim was obviously more comfortable with his daughters. And although we cannot know this as a certainty, Jim probably transferred some of the resentment he had for his father onto his son.

Terry likely was aware of his father's hesitancy at an early age. Although Jim's signals were subtle, emotions are clearly transmitted and received between family members. Less subtle was the obvious attention his father lavished on Terry's sisters. This was observed and agreed upon by the entire family. Probably as an early infant, Terry unconsciously recognized that to get his father's approval he needed to be a girl. Like his father, Terry had not learned to be comfortable with physical play. He had not had the opportunity to become comfortable with aggressive activity or sports. Other boys were more physical than Terry and intimidated him with their aggressive but normal play. At some level Terry decided it would probably be safer if he were a girl. This decision had driven a further wedge between him and his father. A cycle perpetuated itself that tore the entire family further apart.

Over a long period of time, this family made some healthy changes. Jim eventually recontacted his parents, and they even attended several counseling sessions together. Terry's mother intensified her relationship with the girls and quit running interference between her husband and son. Jim and Terry began spending increasingly more time together and eventually even learned how to roughhouse. They simultaneously entered karate and judo training as partners. This gave them an acceptable means of making physical contact as well as providing a block of shared time.

The family made other lasting changes. Jim's relationship with his own parents flourished. The children became acquainted with their grandparents. Through the martial arts, Jim and Terry gained a new level of confidence with their bodies. They became comfortable with physical contact. Terry soon lost interest in women's clothing and quit asking questions about surgical procedures.

Recently I decided to recontact Terry's family. Four years had passed since we initially met. I spoke to each family member separately. It was exciting to hear of their growth and changes. Terry was now a senior in high school. He remembered me, but not why he had come for counseling. According to his parents, there had been no further conversation about becoming a girl. He and his father, in fact, were teaching a martial arts course for fathers and sons only. The family relationships were all very strong.

I asked each member of the family to write me separately and explain what they thought made the major difference. The unanimous response was not counseling but Terry and Dad taking karate together! In follow-up telephone conversations, Terry and his father explained it was the ability to be comfortable with physical contact. That broke down the barriers. It was the therapeutic quality of the magic touch.

Mrs. Grego shuffled slowly into my office. Her eyes were reddened and strained from grieving. I guessed she was in her midsixties.

"I'm all alone now," she announced abruptly. "I have nobody—nothing. I feel terrible." She began to cry and continued for quite some time. Mrs. Grego was alone and lonely. Her social resources were all but exhausted. During the next few hours, she shared with me sixty-three years of beautiful memories. I viewed her comments as gifts, and I undoubtedly benefited far more than she from our time together. I sat spellbound as she told of emigrating from Italy as a child and living through the 1930s in Chicago. The stories by themselves were substance of which movies are made.

During our brief period together, I felt as if I had lived many of those years with her.

Finally she stopped. Her yarn was spun. I sat not knowing what to say and not realizing it was my turn to respond. My mind was focused on the past she had shared with me.

"So what you think?" She interrupted my silence. "You think I'm a crazy old woman who lost her rocker with her parakeet, right? That's what Father Tom says, but he's older and crazier than me." We laughed together.

"No," I sighed. "No, Mrs. Grego. You're not a crazy old woman. It's just a crazy old world we live in, that's all. And it's hard to live in it alone."

I ended up directing her to several groups that provided social opportunities for people her age. I also got her an opportunity to be a volunteer grandmother at a local children's hospital. She ended up spending three days a week rocking and "nussing" babies.

Within a matter of days, we also found a kitten for her to adopt. Weeks later she was healthier and stronger than ever.

The problem I had during our session that day was how to introduce the information to her without having her reject it. I did the best I could.

"Mrs. Grego," I began. "Have you ever heard of a holy kisser?"

IMPROVING YOUR PARENTING ART

1. How important was touching in your family as you grew up?

2. Are you comfortable being touched by a friend or stranger?

3. How could you increase the amount of touching you do with your children or other family members?

PARENTING EXERCISES

1. Read the Bible passages that deal with touch. How can you use touch to promote health and healing?

2. During a conversation with a friend or family member, notice the distance between you. Move closer and observe the other person's response. Move even closer and observe again. Practice focusing on your touching patterns and increasing them by handshakes, pats on the hand or arm, hugs, kisses, and brushing elbows.

The most immutable barrier in nature is between one man's thoughts and another's.

—William James

Communication is something so simple and difficult that we can never put it in simple words.

—T. S. Matthews

The first duty of love is to listen.

—Paul Tillich

Get wisdom, discipline, and understanding.

—Proverbs 23:23

7

Talk and Listen to Your Child

THE INTERCOM buzzer broke my concentration.

"John, you have a call on line three," Polly's voice chirped. "Can you answer it?"

"Sure," I responded, putting my notepad away. "Hello, this is John Baucom."

"John, this is Tom Smith," he greeted. Tom was a man I had met socially several times. We weren't close friends, but we did share a common interest in several civic projects.

"Hi, Tom," I answered immediately. "Haven't heard from you in a while. How's everything going?"

"Not too good right now, John." He sounded rather somber and serious. "I've got some family problems. I don't know if I need to talk to you, or Jill does, or what. We've got some bad problems going on."

Jill was his seventeen-year-old daughter, whom I had met on one occasion. It was unusual for Tom to sound this serious. He was an exceptionally jovial and optimistic person. I had once referred to him as a "back slapper." He seemed to be constantly greeting people, pumping their right hand vigorously with both of his. I knew for him to call me at all, with this kind of revelation, must have been a difficult task.

"Tom, I'm sorry to hear there are problems," I spoke slowly. "If there is anything I can do to help, I'd be glad to. I don't know what's going on, but I'd like the opportunity to help you. You have helped me out a time or two."

I paused and waited for Tom to answer. There was a moment of hesitation as he seemed to collect his thoughts.

"John," he began. "This is very difficult. I'll just go ahead and say it. My wife and I have probably messed up. I'm sure you didn't know this, but Jill got pregnant and we forced her to get an abortion. She didn't want one, but we talked her into it. Now she's not handling it too well at all. Frankly, I'm scared she just might do something weird." Tom stopped awkwardly as if unsure who should speak next. I interrupted the void.

"Have you talked to a physician, Tom?" I knew that it was vital for her to be checked out medically first. "Is she okay medically?"

"Yeah," he answered. "Don Smith looked at her and said she's okay but extremely depressed. He's the one who suggested I talk to you. I hated to because of our friendship. I guess I was just embarrassed to get you involved in all of this. I hate for you to see this side of me." His voice broke off suddenly. It accented the same pain I knew he was suffering.

"Tom," I began hesitantly, "I know this has got to be difficult for you. I'm really sorry. But this could happen to me or Don or anyone else. I would call you under similar circumstances. You're my friend. I want to help. Why don't you bring Jill in, and let's see if she'll talk to me." There was another moment of painful silence, and then he spoke in a rush.

"Do you think you can help?" His words were anguished.

"I don't know. It won't hurt anything," I offered. "I promise you, Tom, that I won't make things any worse. Let me get Polly back on the phone, and we'll get an appointment set up as soon as possible, okay?"

He sighed, agreed, and I transferred his call.

"Polly," I explained, "this is an emergency appointment on line three. I need to see Tom's daughter this afternoon. Do whatever you have to do to make sure I get to see her, okay?"

"I'll take care of it," she assured me.

My jaw tightened as I rested my forehead on the palms of both hands. I slowly began to pray, realizing I'd need help on this case.

BARRIERS TO COMMUNICATION

Although communication is something we all do every day, few of us ever really master the art. This is especially true in families. Expressing ourselves to our own children, and helping them express themselves in return, requires patience and energy on both an intellectual and an emotional level.

In the time you spend with your children it's important to allow them to be expressive. It's also important that you model this art of expression. The child needs to hear you say "I like you. I love you. I'm proud to be your father (or mother)."

On one occasion I talked with a sixteen-year-old who claimed her father had never said "I love you."

"Surely he's said it at least once," I questioned. I turned to her mother. "Mrs. Jones, haven't you heard your husband tell Robin he loves her?"

"Can't say that I have," she responded. "I know he does, but he's just not much of a talker."

I stared quietly, truly puzzled by her reply.

"Well," I asked, "Does he ever say it to you?"

She gazed up at the ceiling. "Well, he did once. I think it was back in 1959 or so."

"Mr. Jones, what do you have to say about all this?" I asked. "Do you love your wife and daughter?"

He stared for a moment, then commented.

"Well, I'm still here, ain't I?"

Good intentions are never enough. Without appropriate expression, love is almost meaningless. As parents, you can provide for your children. You can spend time with them. You can take care of them in a myriad of ways. The paradox is, without appropriate verbal expression, the time you spend is going to be far less meaningful to them. Research indicates such expression may also be healthy for you.

As a parent you need to establish credibility with your child prior to any attempt at serious communication. Your child must believe that you are interested in her personal well-being. Only after establishing this foundation can you begin to communicate on a level of emotional meaning to the child. Even then the process is immensely difficult. This is due to other barriers blocking effective communication.

SELF-AWARENESS

To excel at communication you need to have a high degree of self-awareness. This level of self-awareness is rare. Our pace of life is so fast and our responsibilities so great that we seldom are completely in touch with our inner thoughts and feelings. Our efforts at communication then become more random and less purposeful or consistent. The result is communication breakdown.

Parents, instead of responding to children in a predictable and organized manner, become erratic or illogical. We each have certain personality elements that are known to us and others that are unknown. Children need to have a stable and consistent perception of you as a parent. They need to be able to approach you without being fearful of how you may respond.

One of the most common reasons parents are unable to provide this stability is lack of self-awareness. That is, we typically do not see ourselves as others see us. We tend not to realize the impact our words and actions have on others. For example, a sharp verbal attack on a child can cause deep-seated emotional pain if an apology is not given. Repeated incidents, if not admitted or checked, can close off communication with a child.

MEANING

Meaning is always in people, not in words, so it varies from person to person. This happens because we each live totally different lives, with different interests and backgrounds.

The word *poke*, as an example, spoken aloud can have several meanings, depending on the context in which it's used and the person who uses it. To someone from Louisiana, it is a plant for making a salad. To someone else in the rural southern Appalachians, it's a sack. A person in another setting interprets the word as a jab. A North Carolina hog farmer might interpret it as a piece of meat, as in poke (pork) chop. Actually, each usage of the word is correct in its context.

Another communication problem is the orientation of the communicator. I was speaking to one teenage girl, and she explained that she was really beginning to understand the sport of football.

"Let's see," she thoughtfully explained, "there was a personal foul, but I thought those were in basketball. There was an illegal use of hands, several offsides, and unsportsmanlike conduct."

"That's not football," I replied. "Football is end sweeps, long passes, and safety blitzes. It's power and action, touchdowns, tackles, and contact." I was proud of my description and awaited her response.

"No, it's not," she retorted rather smugly. "I should know, I'm dating the referee!"

Her meaning of football had little to do with the action of the players and everything to do with the referee. Attempting to communicate about football with this teenager meant approaching it from the context of a referee. It made perfect sense to her. But a person with a different meaning (as I had) would find it difficult to communicate with her about the game itself. To her, the referee was much more important. As parents, you often need to focus awareness on your child's meaning if you want to communicate effectively.

TIMING

Related to context use is the issue of time and timing. One of the most frequent communication errors made by parents is in this area. It takes a tremendous amount of time and energy to be just an average communicator. Problem-solving communication demands extra portions of each. Yet, too often family members are guilty of attempting to "cram" an issue of major importance into the ten-minute time slot between breakfast and leaving for school. It just doesn't work.

Timing is often as important as the issue itself. Almost universally, when timing is ignored, the problem becomes much worse. It is counterproductive to communicate on complex issues when little time is available. If there is potential for misunderstanding, it's best to delay the discussion until you have more time.

PROCESS

Other barriers to communication can be found in the process itself. Billy and his father illustrated one barrier extremely well.

"He just makes me feel like he doesn't care about us," Billy said about his father. "He never speaks to anyone when he gets home. It's like he's there, and yet he's not there. I'm not the only one who feels like that. Amy does, too. Just the other day we were saying that probably the only reason he doesn't just go ahead and leave is because of us."

"You're contradicting yourself, Bill," his father interrupted. "You said I act like I don't care and then you say the only reason I stay is you kids. It can't be both ways, Son."

"Wait a minute," I spoke up. "Let's make sure you hear what he's saying before you start correcting the logic."

Billy's father was doing what came naturally for him when threatened. Rather than honestly discuss his withdrawal from the family, he attacked Billy's reasoning. When doing so, he effectively discounted Billy's feelings. His unspoken message told Billy to "shut up and back off." Had I not interrupted, Billy would probably have withdrawn from the conversation and given up. His father used his favorite defense mechanism to avoid the conversation. He attacked how Billy communicated instead of listening to what he was saying. This is a common mistake, and one that only results in alienation and anger.

Focusing on language rather than the message is a similar way to assure negative emotions. When Billy used a swear word in therapy, Mr. Johnson screamed, "Don't use that language around your mother! How many times have I told you not to swear, Billy? You're grounded for a month. You want something to swear about? Then you go swear about that!"

"Mr. Johnson, you're missing Billy's point. First of all, you got distracted from what he was saying and didn't respond to his message. But not only that, now you're grounding him for something he said in therapy. We agreed not to do that. The rule was you could be honest here and say what was on your mind."

"Well, there's another rule that's more important. We have a family rule against profanity, and he'll be grounded for breaking it."

Mr. Johnson was so caught up in the rule that he forgot about his son. Apparently the rule was far more important to Mr. Johnson than either the counseling session or his son's sensitivity. This sometimes occurs in communication. You can get so involved in policy or procedure that people are of secondary importance. This is a dreadful mistake, especially in parenting. The costs are simply too great. Parents should always put their children above formalities or technicalities.

GENERATION GAP

An additional barrier has to do with mere knowledge. Years ago the concept of a generation gap was often discussed. At the time the actual term was even quite popular. We seldom hear the term mentioned any longer, even though it is useful to describe this communication barrier.

Perhaps "information gap" or "language gap" would be more accurate. There is, in fact, a difference in the language children, adolescents, and adults use. There is an equivalent difference in the music, values, and culture. This can often introduce misunderstandings and a lack of shared meanings when attempting to communicate.

One adolescent I met for several sessions in counseling reported himself as drinking rather heavily. He stated precisely that he had not gone straight for more than three days in a row in over four years.

"I don't know," he mused thoughtfully. "I don't even know what it would be like to face life and not be high. I mean, what do you do?"

His question and curiosity seemed genuine. After several hours of discussion, he agreed to attempt going one week without consuming any alcohol.

"For you, Dr. B," he explained. "I'll try it one week. No booze. For real."

"Great," I challenged. "You have nothing to lose."

The week passed without any phone contact. I thought about him several times. Quite frankly, I doubted he could make it. For someone with such a severe addiction, a week is quite long. Regardless of the result, we could use it therapeutically. If he surprised me and succeeded, we could build on it. If he drank and failed, it could be interpreted as a signal he needed to seek more intense help. The next day, however, he surprised me in a different way than I could have predicted.

"Dr. B," he spoke excitedly, "I love you. This is great. I should have given up booze long ago. The stuff's trash, man."

"Did you make it?" I asked in amazement. "Did you go the entire week with no booze?"

"Hey, I said I would." He mocked a hurt look. "You didn't believe me or what?"

"You went a whole week without drinking?" I questioned. "No withdrawal pains, no shakes? What is it—you sneaking Librium or something?"

"No way, man, I don't do that junk." He smiled. "Listen, this is great. Booze really doesn't help anything. I love it. The first couple of days were bad, but after that no problem. And besides, I get much better visuals from my acid. The booze was screwing that up."

"What?!" I demanded more than asked.

"Yeah. The booze was messing up my visuals, you know, the visual hallucinations from acid—LSD. You were right, man. I can live without it."

I had no adequate words to respond. I had obviously missed the greater problem. My focus had been so narrowly centered on drinking, that I had missed the big picture. To him, there was a big difference between drinking and other drug use. To him, drug free meant one drug at a time. His culture was far different from mine. When I didn't mention his other drugs, he didn't even consider abstaining from them as well. The barrier was in our lack of a shared understanding. This frequently occurs in the communication gap.

PRINCIPLES OF COMMUNICATION

The idea of communication is a simple one. It involves successfully exchanging a shared meaning with another person. Sounds elementary, but for some reason it baffles us.

There is a reasonably well-known story about five blind men trying to describe an elephant by touching it. One, holding the elephant's trunk, claims it to be like a large snake. Another, grasping the leg, swears it to be like a tree trunk. A third, stroking the large, thin ear. declares it must be like a large fan. A fourth man leans against the elephant's side and insists it must be like a house. Finally, the fifth man pulls on the elephant's tail and dismisses all other descriptions as wrong. He proclaims that an elephant must surely be like a rope. I have seldom read of an example that illustrates the communication process within families as well as this one does.

LISTENING

Dale Carnegie, the great businessman, was invited to a dinner and reception for a local society woman whom he had never met. When they were introduced, Mr. Carnegie focused a great deal of attention on the hostess. He questioned her about her trip to Africa and listened closely to her responses. "Where did you go? What did you do while you were there? How long did you stay? When did you get back?" After each question Mr. Carnegie would listen and nod. He never spoke other than to focus on her. The following day local newspapers reported the hostess's account of Mr. Carnegie being the "greatest conversationalist in the world." All he did was listen!

Listening is a powerful yet unappreciated art. If you want to be a good communicator, you must be an astute and effective listener. In one of his fables, Aesop tells of a fox who was able to cross the thin layer of ice covering a pond. Other animals before him had failed, even though some were lighter than the fox. The difference, as Aesop later explained, was that the fox listened to the sound of the ice. Similarly, we sometimes miss the sounds of our children. Sometimes these sounds can be alarming. Parents can learn to listen as effectively as did the fox.

One study indicated that the important qualities of a good listener included listening without interrupting, facing the child squarely, and looking her in the eye. When attempting to listen effectively, you must be alert and active. As a listener you have responsibility for absorbing the words, facts, and feelings your child is attempting to communicate. You will not be successful at doing this unless you are actively involved in the process. This requires that you not allow yourself to be distracted by grammar or style, the TV, or other extraneous sounds or activities. To listen effectively is to be absorbed with the speaker in an uncritical way.

You also need to listen for total meaning. The meaning is generally very complex and is found in nonverbal behavior as well as in the words. If your child is shaking or sweating while talking to you, there are some extremely loud nonverbal messages being transmitted. As a parent, you need to hear these messages as well as the more explicit ones. The feeling being communicated by your child is often far more important than the words. A child who is sad or upset because his teacher doesn't like him, doesn't need to hear Dad tell him he's being unrealistic or that it will be okay. The child's total message includes such emotions as sadness, fear, and insecurity. A response is deserved on all those levels.

A good listener also listens without evaluating what is being said. The purpose of listening is to capture your child's meaning and to understand the child. This doesn't require persuasion at all. As a nonevaluative listener, you can create an atmosphere of understanding, warmth, and acceptance. In this environment your child is more likely to open himself up and honestly share his thoughts and feelings. He needs to know it's safe to do so.

Equally important is the ability to not anticipate what is being said, or is going to be said. Finishing the child's statement, either in your mind or aloud, is insulting. You may think you know what the child is going to say next, but this kind of mind reading is confusing and damaging to your child. Caring and sensitive parents will listen for meaning, not for words or logic. If you're giving your child a critique of his speaking skills, you're hurting both yourself and him.

Henry Thoreau once said, "It takes two to speak the truth—one to speak and the other to hear." Your child wants to be heard. One way to assure her that she is heard is to give her feedback. Feedback is the response a listener makes to a speaker, to assure that reception is correct. In this book feedback is used very specifically. It involves the use of several key phrases. The first is "What I heard you say is . . ." The second is "Did I hear you correctly?" In between these two phrases is the technical feedback.

The following conversation is an example of nonlistening and no feedback.

"I don't think my teacher likes me."

"Sure she does, Joe. Would you put the clothes in the dryer for Mom?"

"Well, she never calls on me to answer in class. Today I didn't even get to go to the bathroom. But Candice did."

"Oh, well, maybe you can invite him over sometime after school. Did you put the clothes in the dryer?"

"Mom, I'm hungry. Can I eat?"

"Put the clothes in the dryer and then you can go to the bathroom."

A sensitive parent, who is practicing good communication skills, including feedback, would respond differently.

"I don't think my teacher likes me."

"What I hear you saying is that you don't think your teacher likes you. That must make you sad. Did I hear you correctly?"

"Yeah. I always raise my hand to answer, but she never calls on me anymore. Today I had to go to the bathroom, and she never even called on me. But she called on Candice and Candice got to go."

"What I hear you saying is that you raise your hand to answer her questions, but she doesn't let you. You even raised your hand to go to the bathroom, but you didn't get to go. Did I hear you correctly?"

"Yeah. She always used to call on me, and I got the

answers right all the time. I remember she said she'd only call on me when tough questions came up. She said other people need to learn too. But I still wish I could answer out loud. Anyway, I got to go to the bathroom later. Can I eat now, Mom?"

"What I hear you saying is that you want to eat now. Did I hear you correctly?"

"Yeah, I'm hungry."

An advanced version of feedback is illustrated below:

"I don't think my teacher likes me."

"You sound real sad, Joe. It must bother you to think your teacher doesn't like you."

"Yeah, it does. I always raise my hand to answer, but she never calls on me. I had to go to the bathroom, so I raised my hand; but she never even called on me for that."

"That must have been real uncomfortable. Sounds like she doesn't call on you at all."

"She used to, but she said the other kids need to answer out loud too. If she gets a tough one I get to answer. But I still like to answer out loud. Can I eat now?"

"Sure. What would you like?"

The first version of feedback is the easiest to begin with and the safest. Using the key phrases "What I hear you saying is . . ." and "Did I hear you correctly?" will help you stay on track and let your children know you're listening. In between the two phrases is the substantive feedback. You want to capture the *emotions* as well as the words. Do not add or detract from the message, meaning, or emotion. Try to use words either identical or similar to your child's words. Your attempt is to understand their interpretation, not for them to understand yours. Going back to the previous example, your child says, "I don't think my teacher likes me." If you respond, "What I hear you saying is that you don't like her," you are inaccurate. Don't add your interpretation to your child's message. Understand it and feed it back with *his* meaning.

UNDERSTANDING

To be an excellent communicator you must understand your children. This is achieved by all the things you have discovered up to this point. There are several other vital elements with which you also need to grow familiar. The first is empathy. Empathy is the ability to put yourself in your child's place and experience his meaning as he does. It is an important element in communication, and its absence can lead to an incredible lack of understanding. It is not sympathizing or feeling sorry for your child. More accurately, it is understanding him as he is.

Empathetic understanding enables your child to better adjust her communication in the relationship. It enables her to feel confident, comfortable, and safe to open up with you. It also reduces other barriers that may have built up over the years. It's important that you understand emotions and behaviors that increase empathy.

The first is an absence of negative evaluation. Any nonaccepting response or behavior reduces trust and confidence. Equally as important is time spent getting to know the child as a unique, separate individual. Recalling your own childhood is also very valuable. How would you have felt in similar instances? For empathy to grow, the relationship needs to include supportiveness and equality of value. If your child feels threatened by potential criticism or attack from adults, empathy will never be achieved.

Another characteristic of understanding your child is your willingness to attend to your child's behavior. When any communication of importance occurs, you must tune in to your child's needs at the moment. Experts indicate that some of the following behaviors will help you tune in. When your child is speaking, pay attention. Begin by mirroring her nonverbal behavior. Breathe when she breathes, nod when she nods, and change position as she does. Your language also needs to mirror her language. Her meaning becomes the most important thing in the world. At that moment you are totally attending to your child.

This is an exceedingly powerful way to build rapport with your children. Even before my sons could speak, I would attend to them in this way. On several occasions when they were upset, I would calm them by breathing with them. On several occasions I even took my shirt off and laid them on my chest. I would then begin to mirror their breathing. Within minutes they would deepen their breathing and relax. Soon they would be asleep.

An additional element of understanding is the communication of feelings. Children are discovering new feelings from birth all the way to adulthood. We can help them in this process by discussing our own feelings as well as giving them feedback on theirs. The feelingless Mr. Spock in "Star Trek" is indeed fantasy. Feelings do exist and emotions are going to be experienced. Your children will feel the full range of emotions available to humans. You can be of most assistance to your child by demystifying feelings and talking about them.

One of these ways is to reflect the child's feelings in much the same way you give feedback. There is one difference. In reflecting feelings you can have some interpretive allowance. Your response is not to tell the child what they should or should not feel, but to help clarify those feelings.

As an example, if your child is upset and complaining about school, you might say, "Sounds like you had a bad day today and are angry." Or you might say, "It sounds like you're a bit lonely since we moved and you changed schools." Your response would naturally depend on the setting. The main goal at these times is to clarify feelings. This procedure, however, can also result in increased empathy. My four-year-old has straightened me out several times when engaged in this process.

"Sounds like you're mad at your brother," I suggested.

"No. I'm not mad at him!" He corrects me. "I'm sad at him."

Understandings can also be built through the use of "I" messages. This is a rather simple process but reflects a more complex shift of internal philosophy. Basically, when talking to your child, avoid any message starting with the word "you." This is especially true when you are angry at something and your child is not bothered by it at all.

As an example, one mother reported the following conversation with her fifteen-year-old son who had come home several hours late for Saturday supper. She initially greeted him and found out he was okay. He explained that there was no problem, he had just been hanging out in the mall and lost track of time.

"I am really angry, Steve," she declared with control. "I love you more than you can imagine, but I'm angry because you were so late. I have explained your curfew, I have told you what time supper is served, and I have told you to call. You were right by a pay phone and could have called. This behavior bothers me because I have been worrying since you left. I missed an evening appointment and had to send Greg looking for you. He missed his date. I love you, but I'm not too excited about this behavior."

In this case the mother did a good job of using "I" messages. She could have said a lot of things. Her "I" message, however, was very clear and appropriate. It contained three different parts. It explained how she felt; pointed out the behavior leading up to her feelings; and explained why it was upsetting.

She could have started out by saying, "You are so irresponsible," or by displacing other angry feelings on her son. However, she claimed responsibility for her own feelings. She said "I'm angry," not "You make me angry." There is a big difference. She is modeling self-responsibility for her son and claiming that the anger is hers, not his.

Understanding can also be built through your own ability to be vulnerable and self-disclosing to your children. Many researchers believe the more we reveal ourselves to each other, the more mutual understanding is achieved. I personally think it's important to be as honest and open as possible with our children. This is obviously based on your child's needs and not your own. It's important, as an example, for you as a parent to admit when you make a mistake. It's important to apologize when you're wrong. This not only helps achieve understanding, but also removes any false expectations your child may have toward perfectionism. Short of this, discussing issues of significance with your child and revealing likes, beliefs, and perceptions can be extremely rewarding to them and you.

Finally, to achieve understanding, it's of vital importance to communicate approval. I have seen dozens of people spend years in agony and frustration in quest of the elusive approval of their parents. Some of these people were in their midsixties, and their parents had been dead for years. Often, it would have taken only a few words of love or support to salvage years of suffering and pain. Hearing "I love you," or "I like you," or "You're a good guy," increases self-worth, builds trust, and improves understanding. It can also prevent a near zombielike search for the missing approval.

CONTEXT

Healthy communication requires a "context" where an open and honest exchange of ideas and feelings occurs.

For communication to be totally effective, certain elements are required. There must first be two or more people who are skilled at both listening and speaking. Then, between these people, there must exist a context that is conducive to communication. These conditions are true whether you are describing work groups, families, sports teams, or any other defined group. Such groups create a communication context.

The first factor required for a successful family communication context is that each family member, especially the children, feel worthwhile. For someone to communicate his ideas, he must feel valuable. Good ideas cannot come from someone who sees himself as having no value. Similarly, if your child's self-esteem is low, he will not feel safe or comfortable about the process of communication. In other words, for an environment to be considered safe, your child must have a sense of being valued.

The second factor common to all groups with a healthy context is no fear of reprisal. Group members are not disciplined or punished for expressing opinions honestly. Nothing will diminish a person's willingness to open up more than getting stung every time he does. This doesn't mean, as a parent, you constantly repress your opinion. It does mean, however, that you don't punish your children for expressing theirs.

Families with a healthy communication context allow disagreement. Each family member is recognized as having a unique personality, and each opinion is respected. Disagreement does not have to be negative or destructive. In fact, it can be invigorating and rewarding. One simple way to insure that disagreements are not threatening is to use feedback during the discussion. Before you state your own opinion, however, be certain you understand your child's.

Another factor, obvious in families with healthy communication context, is unconditional acceptance. If this factor is present, your child knows acceptance does not depend on his total agreement with you. He understands his uniqueness and feels accepted and loved as he is. This makes it safe for the child to be straightforward in communication.

The final characteristic of healthy communication context is that people are allowed to be wrong. We all make mistakes, adults and children alike. This can be an asset if you accept the reality and do not constantly remind your child of all his mistakes. By allowing each other to be wrong, we accept our humanness. We also accept reality.

Several months ago we had a birthday party for my two sons. The house was filled with children ranging in age from below two all the way to eighteen. It was an exciting party and quite refreshing to be around such tremendous energy. Toward the end of the party, as some children and parents were leaving, a few adults became involved in a discussion. As one of this group, I soon heard the familiar voice of Keppy, calling me as he ran up the stairs. He came racing around the corner with a look of intense excitement flashing from his eyes.

"Daddy! Daddy!" he panted. "I made a mistake. Let me tell you what happened. It was real neat." The birthday party had been a "Super Friends" affair. Children and parents were invited to come dressed as their favorite Super Hero. I had decided to be Darth Vader. Keppy was Spiderman, and Chip was Superman. Bennie came dressed appropriately as Super Mom. Apparently, Keppy and his best buddy, Josh, had taken off their capes and borrowed several others. They had somehow secured them together and were running downstairs while holding separate ends of their makeshift sheet. Keppy continued his tale, using great animation. "And then we were running and spinning and everything and then we fell down on the floor."

He paused briefly. "And I looked up and we had made a mistake. We pulled all the ice cream and drinks and bowls and everything off the table. Yeah, it was an accident."

During Keppy's explanation, Josh had been standing in the corner shaking his head. "Nope. Not me," he was mumbling. I smiled and told Josh it was okay, then walked over to Keppy. I kneeled down on one knee and began speaking.

"Kep." I pulled him on my knee. "I'm real proud you feel comfortable being honest with me. Thanks for telling me what you did. That's great. I make mistakes too. Now let's you and me and Josh go clean up the mess."

It turned out to be a grand mistake and took several parents as well as two little boys to clean up. However, I couldn't have set up a better learning experience. The context we established was worth the mistake!

As Jill entered my office, I gasped. She acknowledged I was there, then proceeded robotlike to the blue rocking chair. I mumbled a startled apology and sat across from her. We had met before. I recalled her as being a young woman of striking beauty. Several people described her as having a perfect face. She had appeared in several magazines, and although she was only seventeen, she had already earned enough from modeling to buy a small car and pay for her college education.

It was difficult to believe this ghoulish-looking person across from me was that same teenager. Her eyes were swollen but hollow. The hair matted around her cheeks seemed to be almost waxed together. Her hands fidgeted nervously as she began to softly sob and rock back and forth in the chair. Her father had been correct in his description. The abortion obviously had destroyed his daughter.

I sat across from her, rocking in unison and respecting the silence. She cried for thirty minutes. I had only been able to build a thirty-minute emergency appointment into my schedule that day. We still had not spoken. I allowed her to cry and didn't impose any need for her to speak.

"Jill," I finally broke the silence. "I'm sorry to have to go now, but our time is up. I'd like for you to return tomorrow. You have a lot of sadness and we need to look at it some more. I want you to come back.

She made eye contact with me for the first time.

"You probably think I'm crazy, don't you." She stated it as a fact, rather than a question. "I came in here and cried for the entire appointment. You probably think I'm crazy."

"No, I don't think you're crazy. I think you're very, very sad."

As she left, I scheduled her for a ninety minute appointment the following day. She was on time, and even looked a bit better. Entering my office, she began talking immediately, before she said hello or seated herself.

"You must have thought I was crazy," she spoke rapidly. "I came in here yesterday and cried the whole time. I didn't say a word. I know you think something's very wrong with me."

Jill rocked almost manically in the chair. Her rapid-fire, at times staccato speech pattern kept rhythm to the pace of her rocking.

"But I need to tell you what Daddy made me do." She stopped as suddenly as as she'd started. Pausing, she leaned toward me in her chair and lowered her voice.

"You know what he made me do?" she asked. Without waiting for an answer she spoke again. "You aren't going to believe this. He knows I'm a person who saves everything. I've got ticket stubs from the first movie I ever attended. I've got homework papers from the first grade. I've got the first baby doll I ever owned. But you know what he made me do?" She widened her eyes as if anticipating her own response.

"He made me go up there and sweep it all away. Just vacuumed it all up. And now—now—it's all—gone. Gone— forever." Body-wracking sobs erupted once again from within her.

"Jill," I heard my own voice, as if in a dream. "I'm so sorry. I can't believe he did that. That was so stupid." No words could attempt to salve the agony of her heart.

Her disclosure and our brief interchange covered a span of less than three minutes. The remainder of our time together was spent again in nonverbal silence, broken only by her seemingly boundless grief, expressed in deep sobbing and agonizing wails. Silent tears of empathy spilled from my own eyes. Some ninety minutes later she collected herself, rose, and left calmly, apparently more at peace than before.

We visited three more times during the next two weeks. Not once did we overtly discuss abortion, or even use the word. Nor did we mention the reason for her coming to see me. It was unnecessary. This seventeen-year-old girl had done what she needed to do, and used the eloquent language she wanted to use. I have yet to hear a more appropriate use of metaphor and parable to explain a traumatic event.

The following Christmas I received a card from Jill, who was then attending a major university in the South. She said *she was doing extremely well and sent me Christmas wishes. The next summer my intercom rang on a busy Tuesday morning.*

"John, somebody wants to see you," Polly announced. "Can we interrupt you for about five minutes?"

"Sure." I laid my pen down. "Come on in. I need a break anyway."

As I looked up, I saw Jill, obviously older and in good spirits. She had gotten back the perfect face. Once again the description fit.

"Hi," she smiled. "I didn't know if I could see you or not. I'll only take a minute."

"Well, it's good to see you," I answered sincerely. "I didn't expect this."

"I'm doing real well in school. By the way, I'm going to major in psychology." Her face beamed.

"Better major in something at which you can make a living," I laughed. After a few minutes of small talk, I could tell Jill had something serious to discuss.

"Back last year," she began. "When I came to see you back then, you knew what was going on, didn't you?"

"Yes." I confessed. "Yes, I did."

"You know," she shared. "I could tell, somehow. I knew that you knew what was going on. And you didn't make me use those words. You let me talk about it my way. I want to tell you something. You were the only person in the world who understood. If you would have made me say those words I would have never come back. I would probably have killed myself. I want you to know," she smiled, "I love you and I wish you peace."

"Peace to you, Jill." I shook her hand.

"Peace to you, too."

IMPROVING YOUR PARENTING ART

1. Consider which barriers keep you and your children from communicating effectively. For example, is it self-awareness, meaning, timing, process, or generation gap? Decide what you will do to break down the barrier.

2. Of the amount of time you spend communicating with your child, what percentage is spent talking and what percentage is spent carefully listening? If the ratio indicates that you talk too much and listen too little, what will you do to improve it?

PARENTING EXERCISES

To improve your skills as a communicator, practice the following instructions and repeat them as often as needed or desired:

1. Get four 3 x 5 cards. On one, write instructions for week one; write instructions for week two on the second card; and so forth for all four weeks.

2. During week one, carry the corresponding card with you in a pocket or purse at all times. Look at it five times a day to remind you of the instructions.

3. Practice the instruction on card one five times each day for seven days.

4. Repeat step three for cards two through four.

Week One: Concentrate on the adage "Stop, Look, Listen." *Stop* when your child talks to you this week. *Look* into her eyes, focus on her body posture, mirror her posture and breathing as nearly as possible. *Listen* to the message she's sending you. Don't get tripped up by language such as swearing or your own meaning of words.

Week Two: Continue using your skills from week one. Add feedback practice. That is, clarify the message your child is sending by saying first, "What I hear you saying is . . ." and ending with "Did I hear you correctly?" Mirror her words and emotions. Do not include your own response or interpretation during this process.

Week Three: Continue using skills from weeks one and two. Add "I" messages when you respond to her. For example, start your responses with I feel, I think, I wonder. Avoid "you" messages. They tend to trigger defensiveness.

Week Four: Continue using skills from weeks one through three. Add verbal messages of assurance and caring for your child in your responses to him. Remember and share briefly your own related childhood experiences. Let him know you can identify with some of the emotions he is experiencing.

Repeat the entire four weeks as often as needed until you no longer need to carry reminder cards. At that point, you will have made significant progress in the act of parental communication.

GOOD ENDING!

To be a good shepherd is to shear the flock, not skin it.

—Tibertus

But for that very reason I was shown mercy so that in me, the worst of sinners, Christ Jesus might display his unlimited patience as an example for those who would believe on him and receive eternal life.

—1 Timothy 1:16

8

Encourage Your Child to Be Self-Disciplined

AS A BURR-HEADED eight-year-old, I lived in what was then a small city in rural North Carolina. Life was slow-paced but exciting. During this particular time there was a great deal of anticipation in the air as election year approached. The civil rights movement was beginning in earnest. My father worked for an extremely progressive newspaper that provided favorable coverage to the civil rights activists. There was a sense in which we were all on the edge of something very important that was about to explode. In reality it was probably merely the ending of one era and beginning of another, but it was an exciting time.

Life was quite stable in spite of the changes. The community was small and people knew each other by first names or by their parents. I was known as Baucom's boy by community adults. That was fine with me. I had my group of friends and we were able to safely roam the community with a feeling of being accepted and recognized.

One day two of my pals and I decided *we wanted some candy.* But unlike other days, we figured it would be fun to see if we could get away with swiping the candy. We sneaked into the candy section of a local store and ten minutes later were facing a police officer. The officer took us to the police station and began calling our parents.

"What's your name, son?" he demanded sternly.

"Johnny Baucom," I whimpered.

"Baucom, your dad a policeman?" he asked.

"No sir," I sniffled back.

"Who's your dad, son? Whose boy are you?"

"He works for the Daily News," I explained. "But you probably need to call my mom because—"

"Oh!" he exclaimed. "I know your daddy. Big John Baucom—Quincy, right? I've known him for years. Boy, is he going to love this!" The big officer laughed as he picked up the phone.

"Probably you should call my mom." I tried to convince him. But it didn't work. The telephone conversation seemed to last forever. I couldn't hear any of it. Although I assumed he was speaking to my father, I wasn't absolutely sure.

That turned out to be a Friday night I've never forgotten. I didn't watch my favorite TV shows or eat our traditional Friday night banana splits.

This Friday night was different. I spent the night in jail!

BOUNDARY

The term *discipline* originates from the Latin word meaning "instruction" or "to teach." *Disciple* comes from the same root. It implies order, structure, and respect for other people. This is true in life today. As an example, we are a country of law and order. Our behavior is guided by rules. Rules (laws) and consequences for violating them are published long before they're enforced. This gives our society a structure of discipline and appropriate boundaries to protect people. It's actually a good discipline model to follow in our families.

One of the things parents appear to have the most difficulty with today is applying appropriate discipline, structure, and boundaries to their families. As an adult, I know the speed limit is 55 miles per hour in some states and 65 in others. If I forget, the highway is filled with reminders. Every few miles a sign is posted to remind me. I can choose to violate the speed law. If I do, I may also be choosing to accept the consequences. I'm aware of that ahead of time. Citizens violate laws every day. And then they experience the consequences. From this discipline we are educated and taught responsibility and respect.

Similar structure and boundaries are important for a system of discipline in our families. Going back to highway laws is a good way to look at another example. Just as you know the speed limit, you also know the consequences if you break it. And you know these consequences well ahead of time. The boundaries are clear. The law officer does not have the discretion to beat, scream, or ground you because he or she is in a bad mood. The consequences for going fifteen miles per hour over the speed limit are the same every day of the week. There is stability in that approach for you as a driver. You don't have to become neurotically anxious as you drive, fearful of being shot by some policeman who may be having a bad day. If you drove around with that fear, you can be certain it would make a big difference in your daily commute or shopping trip.

In the same way, clear structure and boundaries make life more stable for your children. It may be, especially with an adolescent, that she will not necessarily like some boundaries. Yet, there is still an unspoken comfort in knowing the structure is there. It is frightening for a child to think boundaries do not exist. Not only is there stability in them, but also an equal amount of safety. I have seen dozens of adolescents panic when they realize the safety of boundaries, for whatever reason, is not there.

Healthy boundaries involve consistency of logical rules with logical consequences for violating them. A parent who punishes "as the mood strikes" is providing neither safety nor security. Instead, such inconsistency breeds an environment where confusion and anxiety flourish. This was illustrated during a group discussion after a conference I conducted.

"It's funny," Jack commented. "I knew somebody was crazy. At one moment he was beating the crap out of me. The next minute he was crying and hugging me. I didn't know what to believe."

Jack was describing the way he had grown up. Now a father himself, he was having difficulty setting structure and boundaries for his own children. At times he actually feared falling into the same pattern as his father.

"I mean, there was no way to predict what would occur next," he explained. "One day he actually kicked me because I was watching the wrong channel on TV. I went flying through the air like a football or something. Two or three days later I got in trouble at school for cheating. He ignored it like nothing had happened. At first I figured he was normal, and I was crazy. You know, I was just eight or nine years old."

Jack's is an unfortunate example, but one we can learn from. As an adult he still had difficulty trusting people. He was uncomfortable with any emotions and earlier in his adult life had experienced conflict with authority figures. All of this was directly related to the instability and lack of structure in his home environment. He clearly had learned that it was not safe to trust other people. Now, on a smaller scale he was repeating similar patterns with his own children. Unfortunately, this is fairly common.

Actually, every family has boundaries. Sometimes, they're just not overtly stated. The boundary may be one that is rather vague. In some families, boundaries may take the form of rules. The rules may be written, spoken, or unrecorded in any way.

Yet, they still exist. One couple came to discuss a problem with their seventeen-year-old daughter.

"She's totally out of control," Mr. Williams explained. "We just can't get her to do anything."

"Okay," I responded. "Be more specific if you can. What does your daughter actually do that makes you say that she is out of control? What does out of control look like to you?"

They gazed curiously at each other without speaking; then Mr. Williams turned to me.

"Well, you know what we mean, don't you? She's just incorrigible. We can't get her to do anything. Everything is out of control. She goes where she wants to. She takes the car without asking. She—"

"Wait!" I interrupted. "Excuse me, Mr. Williams. But that's a good one. She takes the car when she wants to?"

"Yes," he sulked. "She just leaves. We tell her not to and she takes it anyway. I mean, what can you do?"

I looked at him and his wife for a moment. "Well," I spoke. "What have you done so far? What do you do when she takes the car?"

"Nothing," he gaped. "What are you going to do, spank a seventeen-year-old, for goodness' sake? We tell her that she can't do it, and she does it anyway. It's that simple."

"Then you have a rule," I explained. "You have a rule that Diane can take it any time she wants to and nothing will happen. Therefore, it's okay. You also have another rule. And it is, Diane can pretend she's in charge of the family, and you two will play along."

Finally, Mrs. Williams spoke up. "Wait a minute, Dr. Baucom." She leaned forward in her chair and began to speak very sternly. "What do you mean by a rule? This is a real problem to us, and if we're telling her in some way that what she's doing is fine, then I want to stop it. What can we do to turn all this around?"

I began a new approach. "Mrs. Williams, what would happen if you or I took someone's car without permission?"

"You mean stole it?" she asked.

"Yes ma'am," I agreed. "To me, taking another person's car without permission, especially if I've been told not to, is the same thing as stealing. What would happen to you if you did that?"

She laughed and then acknowledged, "Somebody would call the police. I'd probably get arrested—or could!" She stopped for a moment and then continued. "That's the only thing I can think of."

"John," Mr. Williams spoke up. "Are you suggesting we get our own daughter arrested for taking the family car? That's a bit absurd, isn't it?"

Before I could answer, his wife broke in.

"Wait a minute, Dick, I think that's right. If she took anybody else's car that's what would happen. We're teaching her to be irresponsible. This makes some sense to me. I think we've been making life too easy on her. My goodness, she'll be leaving home at the end of this school year. She's got to learn respect for other peoples' property someday."

The conversation continued for the rest of our session, but by the end they still had not decided what to do. That appointment was on Thursday. They made a note to call me on Monday and let me know what they were going to do.

On Saturday morning the answering service notified me that I needed to call Mr. Williams. Dialing, I wondered what had occurred. "Hi, this is John Baucom," I spoke. "I had a message to call you."

"Yes," he sighed. "Thanks for calling back. Last night Diane took the car and hasn't returned yet. She said she'd be back this afternoon. What do you think we should do?"

I thought for a moment before answering. "I don't know what you should do. Did you talk to her about any rule changes?"

"No," he answered. "My wife and I hadn't made up our minds until this morning. We're going to call the police. I guess I'll call them after our conversation."

"The thing is," I pointed out, "that she is living by the current rules. I mean, she's been taking the car for over a year and a half, and you haven't done anything. So the rule is, she can do it and nothing will happen. If you're going to change the rule, it might be important to let her know ahead of time. Actually, I'd probably write it up and let her know you're serious. Tell her that the next time she does this without permission, you're going to report the car stolen and let the police handle it. Once you tell her, she'll do it to find out if you're being straight. So if you decide to tell her that, you really need to mean it."

They did mean it. And Diane got arrested. It was the last time she took somebody's car without permission.

STRUCTURE

The purpose of any parenting structure is to help parents produce healthy and responsible children. It is possible that a young child could be internally healthy yet behaviorally irresponsible. In fact, responsibility is difficult to learn. Unfortunately, in our society today it is rarely learned. Yet, appropriate structure can assist in rearing responsible children who will become responsible adults. One way to do this is to provide the child gradual opportunities to experiment with responsibility and authority at an early age. This can begin at birth by providing a participative approach to family living.

The participative approach produces an atmosphere in which parents and children are given mutual respect and consideration. Each member of the family also has to meet certain responsibilities. Parents and children alike contribute their share to family functioning. One's "share" may be different than another's. However, everyone works together for the collective good of the family as a whole. Each family member plays a vital role, and in return is treated as fairly as possible. Some family structures give allowances for fulfilling responsibilities. Others provide no allowance for basic responsibilities, but reward extra tasks with money or extra privileges. The goal in a participative approach, however, is each child learning gradual responsibility.

This approach can be aided by regular family meetings, where members discuss matters that affect the family. It helps if the meeting is democratic in nature with each member allowed to have equal say. Any topic can be discussed in a family meeting. Chores, vacations, or supper complaints are all fair topics. The family meeting provides a unique forum for people to listen to each other's comments. Siblings can learn to understand and respond to each other. Parents can begin to appreciate the unique problems that their children face. It also provides the family an opportunity to regroup and maintain emotional contact with each other.

One father I met with explained that as a child his parents conducted family meetings. His parents discussed job changes, moving, car purchases, and just about everything else with the children. He grew up thinking it was normal to be treated with respect and value. In fact, he was in his late teens before realizing everyone didn't have family meetings. It was not only a forum for communication to this man, but also a vehicle to help increase his self-esteem. Family meetings can do that.

Some people have them at restaurants, and it becomes a special night out. Other families have them at home after a meal. Some families conduct them ritualistically with religious overtones. The specific forum depends on the family. But it's best if the actual business portion of the meeting is democratic and participative. If the parents conduct the meeting dictatorially, it will be self-defeating.

This structured forum can be a tremendous opportunity for your child to begin learning responsibility and discipline. It requires patience, but your relationship with your child will be enhanced, and it will have a major positive impact on their emotional development.

GRACE

On a radio call-in talk show in Chicago, I once received a very angry call. "I think you shrinks are causing more problems than anyone else!" The man spat his words out angrily. "I tell you what kids need today. They need their fannies kicked. I used to beat my kids with a strap, and I never had any problems at all. You're making it sound like it's parents who have all the problems. Well, let me tell you something. You're the problem, not parents. Just do what the Bible says. Beat them with the rod, and they'll turn out fine. My daddy did that to me, and I did it to my children. We turned out just fine!" This caller was using the Bible to rationalize his approach to child rearing. Viewing the life of Christ, however, I find it difficult to support his comments.

Christ's approach was one of forgiveness, mercy, and grace. He constantly presented a model of patience to both children and adults. His attitude toward children, in particular, was one of constant affirmation. And even at the point he was to be arrested, he modeled grace. Peter cut off the ear of one of those coming to arrest Christ. Patiently, Christ rebuked Peter while reattaching the ear. On other occasions, he stressed the importance of patience and empathy. There is no record of Christ as a parent. We can only assume he would have presented the same attitude in that role.

Sadly, too often that is not what we see. The most visible extremes are those of a complete absence of structure and boundaries or else physical punishment so severe that it is practically or completely abusive. Often, a parent will vascillate between these two poles.

Several years ago I was traveling with my family during the Thanksgiving holidays. Bennie and the children slept as I enjoyed the solitude of a quiet, late fall drive. It was a welcome loneliness. My mood was interrupted as a car pulled alongside me on the interstate highway. It was going only a few miles per hour faster than my car and slowly inched ahead of me. What I saw in the car made me almost panic.

In the back seat three children were locked in carseats. They all appeared to be under ten years old. The youngest was probably only five. The child in the middle had his arms crossed in front of his face to avoid the blows he was receiving from a woman I assumed was his mother. He appeared to be crying aloud and was bleeding. The other children attempted to shield him. The mother had turned around in the front seat to face the children. In her hand she held a shoe and was swinging it manically at the child while he screamed.

As I watched, my face flushed with anger. I adjusted my position behind the steering wheel, feeling the heat in my neck and face. My heart began to beat loudly in my ears as I gripped the steering wheel more firmly. I sped up and glared at the car. They didn't notice me! I was surprised they couldn't feel the heat pouring out from my entire body.

Finally, I leaned on my horn and shook my fist at them. The driver sped up, and the woman turned around. He sped up more as I kept pace. By this time Bennie had awakened and quizzed me about why I was driving so fast. I looked at the speedometer while explaining to her and saw that I was going over 90 miles per hour. By that time, the driver had made the woman stop beating the child, but they still refused to pull over or even look at me. Bennie asked what I was going to do if I finally got them to stop. I realized there was almost nothing I could do. I had probably already achieved the only productive goal. As I slowed down they sped away, and I never saw the car again.

What I probably wanted to do was give her husband a taste of the shoe the woman was using against her children. It would have been a stupid mistake. Bennie was more intelligent. She copied their license plate number and reported them to the police when we pulled off at the next exit. Her example was one of grace. Mine was one of vindictiveness.

SELF-RESPONSIBILITY

Extensive research has been conducted on the effects parents have on their child's behavior. Significant evidence has been found that parents who are accepting and provide structure have the most responsible children. These parents emphasize the independence and individuality of each child while simultaneously exercising gentle control. Successful parents are rational and flexible while attending to the child as a unique individual. They seem to value the child's opinion, keep the communication lines open, and try to provide the child with a stimulating environment. Parental control is there, but it is not arbitrary. On the other hand, these parents are not permissive. Clear boundaries and limits are drawn. Yet, the child has freedom to choose within the boundaries. In this way parents become effective role models for the child to follow, and the child learns responsibility in the most effective way.

As a concerned parent, you are interested in how to handle misbehavior. The more you are able to ignore the unacceptable behavior, the better. If ignored, the behavior may go away. In reality, however, such thinking is somewhat idealistic. When your fifteen-year-old is beating up your eleven-year-old, it can't be ignored. In these cases other options can be used.

As immediately as possible you need to interrupt the undesired behavior. If possible, correct the child while he is misbehaving. It is important not to ridicule the child during the correction. It is also very important to separate the misbehaver from the behavior. I have a bias that it is important to sandwich the correction between positive strokes. Nevertheless, the emotion and facial expression need to be serious during the process. The following method seems to work best:

1. Make eye contact with the child, and be physically close during the correction. You may want to place the child in your lap if he is a young child. If your child is an adolescent, get

close but don't violate his "personal territory." This is a correction, not an intimidating challenge.

2. Call him by name and tell him you love him. Let him know how much you care. Assure him of your unconditional love. Separate who he is from his behavior. Express your concern or disappointment in a calm but firm voice. Share your emotions.

3. Point out specifically the observable behavior about which you are concerned. Be as objective and rational as possible in your description. Explain that it's the behavior that bothers you and not the child.

4. Tell the child specifically how you want him to change his behavior and what you want him to do.

5. Ask if there are any questions. Ask him to give you feedback on what you've said. Then let him know what the consequences will be if the behavior reoccurs. Repeat step 2, but alter it to indicate the correction is over.

In action, the correction would be similar to this:

1. You see Corey hitting his brother Brad. You take Corey aside and tell Brad to go and play. You then accompany Corey inside where you both sit on the couch.

2. "Corey," you begin. "I love you a lot. You're a good boy and I enjoy being your father. A moment ago I saw you hitting your brother and I'm upset about that. It really bothers me to see you hit him that way."

3. "You hit him three times and then started to walk off without apologizing. You're a good guy, and you know that kind of behavior is not acceptable."

4. "Number one, I don't want you to pick on him any more, and number two, I want you to apologize."

5. (a) "Do you understand what I'm saying?" (b) "Okay then, give me feedback on what I said." (Father waits while Corey gives him feedback.) (c) "If I see you hit your brother again, I'm going to take away your bicycle privileges for two weeks and not let you play outside for three weeks. It's that important to me." (d) "You're a good guy, Corey, and you

know better than that. So keep up the good work; and if you get to the point where you want to hit your brother again, come talk to me, okay? I love you, Son."

MANAGING BEHAVIOR

Some children need more structure than others and in these cases various behavior management programs can be implemented. Sometimes behavioral contracts or point cards are necessary. These are verbal or preferably written agreements detailing a desired behavior change. They can be as elaborate or simple as you wish to make them. However, they must be understandable to and achievable by the child. Simple discussions of the problematic behavior can be very useful. For children over the age of eight, one of the most therapeutic forms of correction is to require that they write a brief essay explaining the possible negative consequences of their misbehavior.

I received a phone call from a personal friend who had caught his thirteen-year-old daughter lying. He wanted to know the best way to deal with it. I explained to him what I had recommended on several occasions with other families. This involved the "sandwich" correction combined with the requirement of an essay on why it's important to tell the truth.

"How important is it to you?" I asked.

"Very, very important," he replied seriously.

"This can become a big contest," I warned him. "Teenagers can be stubborn. If you tell her to write the essay, she may try to wait it out. Are you in a hurry?"

"No," he replied. "We'll stay up all night if we have to."

He almost did! He asked for the essay at 4:00 P.M. It was after midnight when she finally completed it. But during the process, as a result of the hours they spent in conversation, both agreeing and disagreeing, they became very close. His daughter had an emotional reaction about her propensity to lie and began making significant changes.

On other occasions time out in a quiet room or quiet chair can be a useful process. This involves requiring a young child to get in a particular room or chair as a result of negative behavior. Isolating the child in this way provides an opportunity for him to think about his behavior. For older children, time out can also be a useful tool for allowing the child to calm down. In both cases you place your child in a safe and bland area where there is little stimulation. The amount of time out depends on the child. Two to three minutes is appropriate for a young child. The length of time can extend with age up to approximately ten minutes.

I encourage adolescents to declare their own time outs when they feel themselves getting angry. If they do, you as a parent must agree to leave them alone for the agreed amount of time. At the conclusion of that time (ten minutes as an example), the teen is required to talk about his feelings. Some families believe in this concept so strongly they even design quiet rooms. This is usually a secluded and boring small room with some pillows and possibly a mattress on the floor. In the quiet room, people can scream or get upset and be left alone. There is a time limit, however.

All of these are positive alternatives for discipline. Each has been found successful and useful in teaching responsibility. They're also quite easy to learn and master. It is important that you utilize what works best with your particular child. Some respond more readily to contracts, although others need the time provided by a quiet room. Still other children may want to talk it out with you individually. Some children require more structure. When they do, you may need to resort to a more organized approach.

STRATEGY

"I understand what you're describing in general," the woman spoke up. "But specifically, how do you apply it?"

"Give me an example from your own family," I requested. I was conducting a seminar on the subject of discipline. The question-and-answer period had begun.

"Easy," she sighed. Everyone laughed. "I've got a six-year-old. She won't put on her jacket in the mornings. It doesn't matter how cold it is or anything. If she doesn't want to put it on, she won't."

"What have you tried so far?" I asked.

"Spanking primarily," she admitted. "But it doesn't seem to be doing the job."

"Okay," I began. "Probably it won't. What would happen if you went outside without a jacket when it was cold?"

"I'd get cold," she quickly admitted. "Shiver and shake probably."

"Good," I agreed. "Why not do the same thing with her? She's young. So make a rule. You tell her three times to put on her jacket. If she doesn't do so she can't wear it that day. Let her get cold once. You'll never have a problem with it again."

The next morning it was eighteen degrees outside. I had forgotten the discussion and was more concerned about getting my frozen car started. I found out later, the six-year-old was then being told for the third time to put on her coat. She refused and went outside to catch the bus. Immediately she ran back in and asked for her coat. Mother refused and eventually had to physically carry her daughter onto the school bus. The bus driver scolded the mother and gave the six-year-old her own coat! An hour later the mother got an angry phone call from the teacher.

"Well, there's this guy named Dr. Baucom who said . . ."

In another hour I got a phone call from the school principal! After twenty minutes of discussing discipline, he agreed with me, and several months later I conducted a workshop for his teachers! The bus driver still thinks I'm a jerk, but the six-year-old never again refused to put on her coat!

Occasionally you may have to resort to a highly structured

strategy to help your children control their behavior. In doing so there are several points to remember. The strategy must be as logical as possible. Children can see through elaborate hoaxes. It is logical, as an example, to get cold if you didn't put on your coat. That's rational.

The system must also be based on the child, not a particular person's philosophy or what worked with a neighbor's child. It needs to be child-centered, not theory centered. As a parent, your own flexibility is paramount. If the strategy doesn't work, be willing to throw it out. Your child is far more important than any plan. The strategy also needs to be written down. Share it with your child and agree to try it for a week or two. Then renegotiate.

I have found a four-part system to be most effective in cases where much structure is needed. The first part of the system is family rules and consequences for breaking them. Each child has a different set of rules. The rules are first of all discussed by the parents. After you agree on rules and consequences, you then present them to your children and negotiate. Occasionally your child may have good reasons why a particular rule or consequence is unreasonable. If so, change it. If not, however, enforce the plan.

Make sure the consequences are logical. As an example, one family had a problem with their teenage son failing to turn off his lights. They decided if he left his lights on after going to school, he lost his light bulb for twenty-four hours. If he left his stereo on, the consequence was losing it for the same period. This was an extremely logical approach and had excellent results.

Part two of this system includes expectations and rewards. An expectation is not a rule. It's something you'd like your child to do but not a requirement. However, if he meets the expectation, he gets a certain reward, either points (for teenagers) or tokens for younger children. This does not replace the normal responsibilities your child must meet as a result of being in a particular family. As an example, if Greg's job is mowing the yard, he doesn't get points for it. But if you have an expectation that he'll make As on his report card and he does, then he gets the points.

Part three of the system is simple. Every time you see your child doing something right, reward her both socially and with the appropriate token. Don't wait until she's making a mistake to say something. Give her attention for doing something right!

Part four of the system is the exchange value. Points or tokens are worthless, unless they can be cashed in for something. This can be extra privileges, money, or whatever you know will motivate your child. As an example, if your child likes to play on the computer, thirty minutes of extra computer time costs fifteen points. If your child likes to go to a movie, that costs forty-five points. This must also be individually based on your unique child and the point system you adopt.

Looking back, jail wasn't so bad. I was separated from other "inmates." Different deputies talked to me at various times, and the food was good. Nobody bothered me. Nevertheless, at the time I was scared to death! Saturday was the longest day of my young life. No cartoons, no pancakes. I felt abused. During lunch a policeman came and opened my cell door.

"Somebody here to see you, Son," he said, smiling. "Come with me." He placed his huge hand on my shoulder and directed me into an office. My father was there laughing and speaking to the desk sergeant. He looked at me and smiled.

"We'll see you guys later." He waved. "Thanks."

"Quincy, you and your boy come back and see us," the sergeant called out.

Not me, I thought to myself. I'm never coming back to this place again.

Dad was holding my hand, but he hadn't spoken to me yet. He opened the door to his Studebaker Lark, and I crawled in. He silently followed and seated himself behind the steering wheel. He turned the switch and then pushed the ignition button. The car fired and began rumbling noisily. He put the car in gear and then paused.

"Son," he looked at me warmly. "What happens when people break the law?"

"They go to jail, Daddy," I whimpered.

"Did you break the law?" he asked gently.

"Yessir," I sobbed.

"Did you go to jail?" he asked.

"Uh-huh," I nodded, almost out of control.

He paused a moment longer.

"Are you ever going to steal again, Son?" he asked.

"No sir," I blurted out. I could no longer hold back the tears.

"It's okay, Johnny," he said. "I'll never mention it again." And he didn't. Nor has anyone else ever mentioned it in my family. The experience itself said enough. I found out later that this experience caused a major problem between my mom and dad. Our minister tried to get Dad to let me out of jail, as did my grandparents. But he stuck by his decision. Apparently, he believed quite strongly in what he was teaching me.

Some people have said he had a premonition of his early death. Others say it was just the way he was. Whatever—I'm grateful. He died a year later. And I still miss him.

IMPROVING YOUR PARENTING ART

Guidelines for Teaching Self-Responsibility

1. To teach a child self-responsibility, logical or natural consequences should immediately follow the related behavior.

2. Parents decide on specific rules and related consequences for each individual child. These need to be written out and posted. To make sure that each child understands both, have each child state them back to you.

3. Implementation of rules with consequences must be consistent and firm, yet merciful.

4. Family meetings can be a vehicle for improving family communication and cooperation. To be effective, they must be democratic; each family member must be allowed to share thoughts, feelings, and ideas. The location, frequency, and agenda of such meetings is unique to each family.

5. Use of the "sandwich method" works best for consequence implementation: (1) verbally assure the child of your love; (2) correct the child; (3) assure the child of your love again.

Behavior Management Techniques

1. *Time Out.* Have the child sit quietly in a chair or stay alone in a room for a prescribed time period that is appropriate for the child's age: up to one minute for very young children; 10–15 minutes for older children; indefinite time periods for teens. Discuss feelings at the end of each time-out session.

2. *Written Essays.* Have the child write a 3-to-5-page essay, to be finished before any privileges are allowed, that explains the negative consequences or dangers of his behavior. Discuss it with him when he has completed the assignment.

3. *Behavioral contracts or point cards.*

4. *Spankings.* To be effective, spankings should not be the primary or frequent choice of intervention. Parents should decide and write down when spanking will be considered appropriate, for what ages it will be appropriate, what part of the body will be contacted, how the body will be contacted, the specific number of times the body will be contacted, and who will administer it. Parents must follow these self-set guidelines.

A person who doubts himself is like a man who would enlist in the ranks of his enemies and bear arms against himself. He makes his failure certain by himself being the first person to be convinced of it.

—Alexander Dumas, The Three Musketeers

Love your neighbor as yourself.

—Matthew 22:39

If you love someone you will be loyal to him no matter what the cost. You will always believe in him, always expect the best of him, and always stand your ground in defending him.

—1 Corinthians 13:7, The Living Bible

9

Build Your Child's Self-Esteem

I SAT HYPNOTIZED by the evening news broadcast. The picture on the screen echoed hauntingly, a kaleidoscope from years past. Was it Greensboro, Selma, or Little Rock? Perhaps it was a rerun of a fifties or sixties news reel. The fact that it was indeed 1987 and occurring only fifty miles from where we sat appalled me. Chip's question brought me abruptly back to the present.

"What's that little boy wearing, Dad?" he questioned innocently. "Is it a karate outfit or what?"

I looked back at the television screen. A toddler staring at the camera was wearing the familiar but ghostly white robe of a Ku Klux Klansman. Several men circled him like vultures, pointing and screaming at the reporters. I glanced down at Chip, with no idea how to respond.

"So what is he, Dad?" He looked at me quizzically. "Is he a Ninja, or ghost, or what?"

"Oh yeah," I said. "I think he's probably dressed up like a ghost."

"Is it Halloween?" Chip asked excitedly.

"No," I confessed. "Not Halloween."

"So why is he dressed up like a ghost?" Chip stared at me intensely. "Is he trying to scare somebody?"

"Probably so," I answered. "Yeah, he's probably trying to scare somebody." As the news broadcast continued, I began wondering how I could explain racism and prejudice to a child.

"Is he afraid somebody's going to get him?"

"No, Son," I sighed. "I don't think he's scared somebody is going to get him. I think he's just trying to act like his daddy."

"What's his daddy scared of?" The predictable questions continued.

I stopped for a moment before answering, then turned toward my son. "His daddy is probably scared of what he doesn't understand. I think he's scared of the unknown. Scared of people he hasn't met. Scared of progress. So he dresses up like a ghost to scare it all away."

"Does the ghost outfit make him brave?" Chip pressed.

"No, Chip." I shook my head. "He's still scared. He's just trying to hide it, that's all."

SELF-CONFIDENCE

Since 1978 I have been the proud owner of two Doberman pinschers. One is a powerfully built one-hundred-pound black-and-tan male named Pharaoh. He is a bright and courageous animal who graduated at the top of his class in both obedience and protection training. However, he also has an instinctive sense of judgment that can't be taught. He can intuitively tell the difference between someone who is a threat and someone who isn't. It so impressed his trainers that they once offered us several thousand dollars for him.

Once we were visiting my mother and had taken Pharaoh

with us. I was reading the paper while Pharaoh lay between my legs, snoring loudly. Bennie had her back turned toward us as she leaned over to change television channels. Meanwhile, unknown to me, mother had spotted a fly in the room and picked up a fly swatter. The fly landed on Bennie's back. Mother began inching closer to Bennie to swat it, her arm cocked for the assault.

Suddenly I heard my mother shriek. I jumped up, dropping the paper. In the scene before me, Pharaoh's forepaws were planted firmly on Mother's shoulders. In his mouth he gently held the wrist of her hand still holding the fly swatter. Other than Doberman slobber, there was no damage. He had not placed any pressure on Mother's wrist, but he wouldn't let her withdraw it until I ordered him to release her.

"Get him off me, please," Mother begged.

"Good boy, Pharaoh," I praised him. "Out! It's okay." Pharaoh let go and then sat beside Mom, still keeping his eyes on her.

Later, as we discussed the episode, we realized what had happened. Pharaoh wasn't going to allow Mother to hit Bennie with the fly swatter! At the same time, he seemed to know that she presented no real threat. Pharaoh always seems to know the difference.

Our other dog, Chianti (we call her Shanty), is a small, wine-colored female who probably weighs less than fifty pounds. At times, I can't believe we actually paid for her. We bought Shanty because Pharaoh seemed lonely. And if opposites really do attract, this relationship should be perfect. Pharaoh is strong, courageous, and intelligent. Shanty is hyperactive, insecure, and fearful. She barks at the wind, and is scared of cats, birds, and people—frightened of anything. She "complains" constantly, and often awakens the neighborhood at 1:00 A.M. with her loud barking and growling at imaginary ghosts.

When Shanty eats, she guards her dish protectively and glares at anyone who dares come close. At times she has even attacked Pharaoh for simply looking in her direction during mealtime!

In spite of her size and insecurity, Shanty is far more dangerous than Pharaoh. She's dangerous because she's frightened. And she's frightened because she's weak. Pharaoh has nothing to fear. He's strong and confident and can easily defend himself if needed. Shanty, on the other hand, has almost no confidence. So she barks, growls, and jumps up and down to keep people away from her. To put it in human terms, Pharaoh has relatively high self-esteem. His behavior implies, "I'm okay, and I'm not scared of anyone hurting me, so there's no reason to act aggressively." Shanty's behavior, on the other hand, implies just the opposite. Fearful of being hurt in some way, she appears aggressive to keep people away. It's all an act, of course.

STRENGTH

I have been told it was Leo Raulston who said, "It's the weak who are cruel. Gentleness can only come from the strong." John Talbird, an Episcopal priest, once suggested a similar sentiment. "Love comes only from strength," he said. "The fearful can experience dependence. But they'll never come close to knowing true intimacy." Thoughts such as these have influenced the personal approach I take toward rearing my own children. I want them to love and to experience peace. Yet, I believe these emotions can only come out of strength and health.

I spent five years of active duty and five years of reserve duty in the military. Part of that time was in combat. I also have dozens of friends who have seen active duty in World War II, Korea, and Vietnam. While in the Marine Corps, I served with men who had fought in World War II and Korea. One friend, now deceased, fought against the Russians in Hungary and against Cubans in Africa. Interestingly, none of those who experienced combat liked it. War is an abomination.

Beyond a doubt, the most pacifistic people I have ever met are military officers who have been in combat.

I abhor war, violence, and pain. It repulses me, as it only can someone who has personally suffered such horrors. As a young paratrooper during the Vietnam war, I was in two helicopter crashes, was wounded twice, contracted malaria, watched my best friend die, and then returned home with the shame and guilt experienced by veterans of that conflict. Having known both horror and violence, I detest them. I want a life of peace and joy, which are by-products of love.

This does not mean, however, that I value weakness over strength. On the contrary, these desirable qualities can only come from strength. And strength comes from self-confidence, and self-confidence comes from self-esteem. This same analogy applies on the family level, especially with children.

I want these qualities for my children. I want them to be strong in every way. I want them to face obstacles with strength that grows out of healthy self-confidence and self-esteem—whether those obstacles are physical or emotional. If they're not intimidated by a bully, they will never have to hurt the bully to get away from him. If they are successful in facing physical obstacles, they will more easily deal with emotional barriers. The child who gives up when a soccer game gets tough is more likely to give up as an adult when marriage gets rough. Therefore, I view persistence and determination as important qualities for my children to develop. If surrounded by water, I want them to swim. If faced with snow, I want them to ski. If there is a mountain in their way, I want them to climb it or go around. So I decided long ago to face such obstacles with them until they can face them alone.

I taught my two-year-old karate, and I put on boxing gloves and sparred with my four-year-old. I have also done this with other children and family members. We don't do it in anger. Nor is it intended to resolve conflict, settle family problems, or teach them martial arts. Instead, the purpose is to help them develop self-esteem.

I have come under fire from some of my friends, who are also parents, for encouraging this kind of behavior. However, the proof is in the results. And in the long term, by helping them learn not to fear obstacles, known or unknown, I can encourage them to develop self-confidence. Out of this will grow self-esteem, the ability to love themselves. And when they can love themselves, they can love others. At that point, gentleness will be allowed to flourish.

SIGNIFICANT EXPERIENCE

It was the last soccer game of the season for the "elfs" league. Keppy had been sick for several days and seemed rather apathetic about playing.

"Whether or not you play is up to you," I told him. "But this is the last game of the season. You won't get to play again until the fall."

"Well," he sighed, "I guess I'll go ahead." It turned out to be his best game of the season. He played vigorously and was exhausted after it was over. On the way home, I complimented him on his game.

"I'm proud of you, Kep," I said. "You played a good game today. And I'm proud of you for going to the game. I know you didn't feel well."

"You know what, Dad?" he said. "I'm proud of me too!"

"Me" is an important concept for a child to develop. It is at the core of personality and is the origin of personal identity. This sense of self is composed primarily of the various roles your child plays and the qualities or characteristics he believes he possesses. At the time of birth, there is no true sense of separateness. In most infants a true recognition of personal identity or separateness from others doesn't appear until around the age of two. Only in the following years, however, does a true sense of self-esteem begin to develop.

Dr. Charles Horton Cooley suggests that self-esteem is really a social product and is determined by a series of social interactions. Cooley's central theme is what he calls the "looking-glass self." He says that society is like a social mirror in which we observe others reacting to us. Thus, according to Dr. Cooley, the self-esteem level of a child is determined by what the child sees. Through the reactions of others, a positive or negative opinion of self is formed. If the "looking glass" reflects favorable images, the child develops high self-esteem. If, on the other hand, the child sees only unpleasant responses, low self-esteem is formed. The images mirrored to a child actually consist of the reactions of his or her parents combined with the reactions of significant others. These reactions are often referred to as verbal and nonverbal "messages."

A message can be a phrase, a look, or an attitude. Children are normally quite sensitive and perceptive. You can communicate self-esteem to them by mirroring approval and praise. "You're a good girl," "That's great," or "Way to go" all build high self-esteem. Nonverbal responses such as smiles, nods of the head, and applause do likewise. It's important for parents to present a positive looking glass to their children.

Both Cooley and his colleague George Herbert Meade discussed the importance of literal and symbolic interaction in shaping a child's personality. As these interactions grow more intense and meaningful, they have a major impact on a child's self-esteem. Such significant emotional experiences can be long-term relationships or unexpected intense momentary incidents. Yet, they not only have a major impact on personality development but also actually change it. In fact, beyond early adolescence significant emotional experience is practically the only way to change personality.

As an impressionable nineteen-year-old in Vietnam, I developed a relationship with a Hungarian refugee over twice my age. I needed a father figure at the time and apparently he needed to parent someone. The relationship developed into a significant emotional experience for me. Naturally, the significance was enhanced due to the intense setting. Nevertheless, the relationship alone would have been significant enough, without the stress of combat. During the time we were together, I began to dress, walk, and talk like him. Soon I was even imitating his accent! I no longer walk, talk, or dress like my friend. But today, almost twenty years later, I am still influenced by his values.

Some years ago, I developed a similar relationship with a young man in my Sunday school class. Our friendship began when he was in his early teens and continued throughout his adolescence. Eventually he became more like a family member. I constantly encouraged him to achieve his potential in anything he attempted. Although I tried not to let my encouragement develop into pressure, at times he probably perceived it that way. He began emulating my behavior: he played football, lifted weights, and copied my style of casual dress.

On several occasions through the years we discussed the possibilities of college, athletics, and future career options. It was clear to me, by this time, that our relationship had become a significant emotional experience for this teenager. He viewed me as a role model. It became painfully evident his last year of high school.

"I've decided I'm going to be like you," he said one day.

"Oh, yeah." I smiled. "In what way?" I assumed he was ready to tell me he'd decided to play college football.

"I'm going to go about life the hard way."

"What?" I said. "What are you talking about?"

"Well, first of all I'm going to go in the Marine Corps. Then I'm going to get the same training you did. Then I'll find some sort of small war. After that's over, I'll go to college and play ball." He smiled proudly.

"Oh, no," I groaned. "I hope you can be talked out of that."

This is the power of modeling. Rather than doing as I had said, he was going to do as I had done.

Perhaps the best thing you can do for your child's self-esteem is to model it yourself. It's the best of all possible looking glasses to hold up to your child.

SELF-ESTEEM

Tim sat in my office across from his parents. Due to his heavy football workouts over the past five years, he was a huge, muscular teenager. His growth had also been stimulated by the abuse of steroids. Although suspicious for quite some time, his parents had only recently verified Tim's drug use. To say they were concerned would be a gross understatement.

"If it were not for the steroid use," I asked, "what else would you be concerned about as far as Tim goes? Grades? Interpersonal conflicts? Is there anything else going on?"

The parents gazed at each other for a moment. "Well," his father spoke first, "I'm not too crazy about his haircut. But other than that we really have few problems."

Tim had gotten a version of the "Boz" haircut, modeled after linebacker Brian Bosworth. On one side of his almost shaved head, hair had grown out in the figure of his football jersey number; on the other side was the letter "M" signifying his high school.

"Yeah," I laughed. "It seems to be the craze right now among football players. What do you think?" I teased. "Look good on me?"

Actually, Tim's family was relatively problem-free. In spite of Tim's steroid use, he was basically a happy teenager, and appeared to be free of stress-related symptoms. His parents were pleasant people and seemed to communicate well.

After we had dealt with Tim's steroid use, I asked Tim's parents about their approach to child-rearing. At first they denied having any one approach, but after some encouragement they agreed to think about how they had reared Tim and discuss it with me.

"I think it was more in the attitude we had than anything else," Tim's mother began as we talked over the phone a week later. "Basically, we loved Tim and really wanted him to know it. From birth he was exactly what we wanted. It was almost like we ordered him from a catalog. He was a beautiful baby boy and very lovable. We were so glad to have him. He hardly ever gave us any problems. His daddy just thought Tim walked on water. They have been buddies and played ball together from the very start.

"We never had to put much pressure on Tim. He just kind of did what we expected without big problems."

I interrupted her. "What was the attitude that you referred to earlier? I guess I'm wondering what you thought or did that made a difference for Tim. You know, if you were telling somebody how to raise a child, what would you tell him? Let's say Tim was getting ready to raise his children. What would you tell him to do, or not to do?"

After thinking for a moment she responded. "I'd certainly say communicate with them. Talk to them like human beings, like they have some sense. I see so many parents talking down to their children, and I've never thought that was any good. I think talking to them is important. And listening to them too. But listen to them as if what they have to say is important. My husband and I both spent a lot of time having conversations with Tim. If he wanted to talk, we would stop what we were doing and listen to him. We figured it was that important.

"I'd also say just let the children be themselves, even if it's not what you'd first want. You know, we didn't like Tim's haircut, but we didn't make a big deal about it. We also don't like some of the language he uses, but we try to let the small stuff go. We realized a long time ago that you can't control everything children do.

"I think all of this helped us understand Tim. But that has been the most difficult part. Really understanding any teenager, I guess, is near impossible, but it's important to try, at least. We think so, anyway."

She paused again, so I spoke up. "You did have rules at home and still do, is that right?"

"Oh, yes," she exclaimed, "yes, indeed. We have a pretty strict set of rules and always have from as far back as I can remember. We probably had more rules than most other folks I knew. But we seemed to have fewer problems too. I think Tim just didn't have a lot of gray areas. We tried to make it clear what was right and what wasn't, so he didn't have to worry about it.

"Really, we never had many problems with rules. Like I said, we told Tim when he was right and told him when he was wrong. We always let him talk about it though. And we would give him a chance to explain. If he thought we were wrong, we let him tell us. Sometimes we were wrong and he was right.

"But mostly we just loved him. He's been a delight to raise in spite of the disappointments. I didn't really care that much about the steroids except that it's bad for his body. I'm convinced of that after talking to Dr. Burns.

"I don't think there's a magic formula for raising children so that they feel good about themselves the way Tim does. To me, it's just love your children, talk to them, let them know what's right from wrong, treat them fairly, try to understand them, and give them a lot of attention when they are doing right. To me, that's about all there is to it."

"Sounds like a formula to me," I said, half-jokingly.

"Well yes," she shyly admitted. "I guess it is."

This mother's common-sense approach to increasing her son's self-esteem may not appear extremely scientific. Yet her commentary is similar in many ways to the well-researched ideas of social psychologist Stanley Coopersmith. Coopersmith, who conducted an extensive study with parents of ten-to-twelve-year-old boys, found that certain parenting practices may contribute to a child's self-esteem. Among these were acceptance and approval of the child, clearly defined boundaries and enforced limits, willingness to listen democratically to the child, and respect for the child's individuality and uniqueness.

Dorothy Briggs supported Coopersmith's postulates and expanded on them. She stated that positive parental evaluations are the primary source of child self-esteem. This is passed on not only verbally, but through physical contact such as hugging. Praise, however, appears to have the greatest impact.

Briggs went on to say that intense encounters in a safe emotional atmosphere also promote high self-esteem. During these encounters children and parents share direct one-on-one personal involvement. This involvement is made safe through several qualities Briggs found to be highly important.

The first of these factors is interpersonal trust. This is different than trusting parents to take them to school or cook supper. According to Briggs, trust is conveyed by the child perceiving that the parents mean what they say. In other words, the child believes that the parents are basically being honest. Certainly, if you're scowling with anger while claiming, "I'm not angry," you are not conveying honesty. Briggs suggests that parents avoid any discrepancy between what they say and what they portray nonverbally.

The second quality is a non-judgmental attitude. This can be communicated by separating the behavior from the behaver. Similarly, sending "I" messages and making statements rather than asking questions is helpful in presenting a non-judgmental attitude to your children. Any blunt criticism can be perceived as a judgmental attitude. There is nothing inappropriate about instruction or correction, but it needs to be done in a non-judgmental way.

Briggs described the third self-esteem building quality as the capacity to cherish children. This involves an unconditional love. Basically, it's loving the child and caring for her just because she is. To cherish your child is to respect her separateness and differences. You focus on her strengths rather than weaknesses and overlook minor irritations. As an example, it was important to Bennie that our children dress up for church. However, Keppy, at age three, decided he wanted to wear what his friends wore. So he presented himself to us on Sunday morning in a football jersey and sweat pants. After some discussion and a great deal of hesitancy Bennie compromised. The truth was, at his age it really didn't matter what he wore to church. And he was correct. Dressed in sweat pants, he actually blended in with his peers. Rather than imposing her own needs on Keppy, Bennie cherished him and respected his separateness. And she was able to do this in spite of the fact that she didn't agree with his choice of clothing.

The fourth quality is the ability to allow your child to experience his own feelings. Although this cliché is overused among those in the helping professions, it is indeed an important attitude. Recognizing that we each experience life differently is extremely important. As a parent, you may be amused by a situation, whereas your child may be deeply hurt. Something that angers a first grader can be irrelevant or trivial to an adult. We each experience a different emotional reality. This is especially true between children and adults. To deny a child his feelings, is to deny his reality. Denying anyone his reality is another way of inducing insanity. It's like telling someone everything he experiences is wrong. To encourage self-esteem in your child, allow him to experience his own feelings.

Briggs's final quality necessary for building self-esteem is a parent's faith in the child's capacity to grow, change, and improve. This is a realistic optimism, based on the awareness that we all can develop to a higher level. Obviously, this requires work. As parents, we have the responsibility of attempting to provide an environment in which such growth can occur. Just as a child's body will grow if provided with proper amounts of food, exercise, and health care, so will her personality. By following the guidelines described, you will increase the probability that your child will develop high self-esteem.

SHAPING SELF-ESTEEM

Self-esteem is not something your child is born with. It is learned, and can be learned by anyone. As Cooley's "looking

glass" theory indicated, all that's required are positive responses from the environment. The most meaningful of these
responses are the significant emotional experiences referred to
earlier.

As an adult, your identity and self-esteem usually come
from within. You like yourself because of who you are, not
what you do. With children, however, that's not the case. Their
self-esteem is affected by what they do. For some, self-esteem
comes quite easily. For others it takes extravagant encouragement. It is similar to the identity crisis teenagers experience:
their self-esteem is determined by the group they belong to, the
clothes they wear, and the car they drive. The group, the
clothes, and the car make up who they are.

For example, the Boz haircut gave Tim an identity
(football-athlete) and correlating self-esteem. The Peters family
is a single-parent family consisting of Joan, the mother; Tim,
her thirteen-year-old son; and Janet, a sixteen-year-old daughter. At our first meeting Joan had some of the same questions
most single mothers do.

"I don't know," she sighed. "Timmy just seems too
passive. He's a big boy, but I feel like he gets run over by his
friends. He never seems to stand up for himself. He's playing
basketball but he seems real timid. I guess it's my fault in a
way. He's never had a good male role model since the
divorce." Joan was experiencing the guilt often reported by
single parents when their children have problems. She was
blaming herself for something out of her control.

"Rather than trying to find blame," I began, "let's see what
we can do to improve the situation. Look at what you've got
going for you. Your son is already expressing interest in sports
activities. That's a terrific resource for building self-esteem."

Sometimes it's only necessary to organize and utilize those
potentials already evident. Timmy was quite tall for his age,
and several teachers had been encouraging him to play
basketball. What he lacked, however, was assertiveness and
confidence. We decided to build on the potential already there.

"Remember," I told her, "for Timmy, self-esteem comes basically from what he does and how good he does it. He learns from that and from how people respond to him as a result of his efforts. It's a gradual process, but eventually he figures it out—I'm okay. I'm all right—and ultimately he'll incorporate that into his personality. But it's going to take some time and effort on our behalf to get that rolling."

In time, many things changed. I taught Joan about the family and home conditions that foster self-esteem. We enlisted a network of other adults to become involved with Timmy, and we built in several positive reinforcement systems to elicit certain behaviors from Timmy. This included paying him money for fouling out or for shooting air balls to encourage him to be more active and assertive during the game.

Timmy also started taking trumpet lessons. This gave him a sense of mastery over his environment. He became involved in an active Sunday school class at a local church, where he established a rewarding friendship with a youth minister. Before the school year was over, Timmy had forgotten why the Peters ever came to see me.

"I guess we were having family problems or something." He shrugged.

"Yeah," I agreed, "I guess probably so. Nice that they're worked out, huh?"

"Let's go shoot some baskets," he suggested.

ADAPTATION

Christ told us to love our neighbors as we love ourselves. This seems to imply that self-esteem is vital if we are to love someone else. Here and elsewhere in Scripture Christ reflects the need for a sense of self-esteem. But the Scriptures also speak of the folly of vanity, and we need to be aware that there is a great difference between the two. Self-esteem is not boastfulness or false pride. It is an accepting awareness of your own strengths and weaknesses, and it is not easily or quickly developed. It takes time for your child to adapt her level of self-esteem to the mirror with which she is presented. She will learn to have high or low self-esteem. But ultimately she will adapt. All people do. So do animals for that matter.

A friend of mine works for a veterinarian and often discusses the personalities of certain animals she has gotten to know through the years. She was particularly amused with what she described as an "obnoxiously loud" tomcat who was brought to the clinic every six months or so.

"You would not believe this cat!" she exclaimed. "He must be going for an Academy award or something. He howls like a dog. He doesn't meow—he howls. It's incredible. But not only that, he actually acts it out like he's playing charades. He'll get right in front of you and jump around till you pay attention. It's really something."

On several occasions she invited me to come by her office when the cat was scheduled for an appointment. Finally I gave in and agreed to meet Oscar, the "famous howling tomcat of Hixson," as they called him.

I knew it was Oscar the moment he entered the office. He strutted confidently through the door on a leash, stopped, and took a proprietary look around the office. His owner was a small woman who appeared to be in her early sixties. There was no doubt who was in charge. Oscar was definitely taking his owner for a walk!

"Must be a watchcat," I mumbled. He was the largest domestic cat I had ever seen. "Steroid freak," I whispered to my friend.

"Hi, Oscar," she called out to the cat. He bellowed back his responsive meow. It was as loud as he was big.

"Goodness!" I exclaimed. "Ma'am, where in the world did you get that cat?" I asked Oscar's owner.

She looked up and stared blankly at me, then realized I must be talking to her. "I'm sorry," she said. "Did you speak to me? These darn hearing aids are acting up something terrible. I don't even wear them at home." She brushed the gray hair off her ears, pulled one of the hearing aids out, and began tapping it to adjust the volume. "These things are just about worthless," she continued. "There's not much worth listening to anyway, is there, young man?" She looked up at me as if awaiting a response.

"Uh—no—I don't guess there is. Really." I laughed. "By the way, have you had those hearing aids ever since you got your cat?"

"Oscar?" she asked. "Oh, I've had him only for about ten years. I've never been able to hear very well. I've had hearing aids all my life. Why did you ask?"

"I just wondered," I said, raising my voice just short of yelling. "Do you think he's loud? I mean, do you think he meows unusually loud or anything?"

"No, not really," she shook her head. "Just like any other animal, that's all. He's just an old tomcat." She took her other hearing aid out and began adjusting it. "He eats a lot, though," she commented. "He'll eat anything. Mostly baby food. Still drinks milk too. He likes sardines and tuna and oatmeal, of all things. Why? What do you feed your cat?"

"Oh, cat food." I smiled.

"Huh?" She strained, bringing her hand up to her ear. "What did you say again?"

I smiled and shook my head.

Oscar was loud. But more than that he was smart. He had adapted to his environment. He had learned to do whatever necessary to get his owner's attention. And his self-esteem had adapted along with his personality. He was as confident as he was loud. Oscar had perfectly adapted to his environment, both in voice and self-esteem.

I turned to my friend. "I've got a Doberman I'd like Oscar to meet."

We sat at the supper table having our customary chatter. "Hey, Mom," Chip said. "Daddy was teasing me about this kid on television. He said the kid was wearing a ghost outfit because his daddy was scared. Isn't that funny?"

"Yes, Son," Bennie agreed. "That's funny." Then she turned toward me. "What's he talking about?" she whispered.

"Well, there was a kid on the news dressed in a Klan outfit. And we were talking about why he would wear that kind of stuff. It became a conversation about fear and—"

I paused. Bennie and Chip were staring at me intently while Keppy obliviously continued to eat.

"Chip, why don't you tell Mom why the little boy dressed up like a ghost," I suggested.

"Well, see," he began, motioning with his hands, "there was this little kid and his daddy had a ghost outfit. I thought it was a karate outfit. But it's not. And his daddy is scared because he doesn't know everything. Then there's these people and he's scared again. So his daddy puts on this ghost outfit to scare everybody away. But the daddy's not really brave. Then the boy dresses up like his daddy. But he's not scared. He just wants to dress like his dad. Then there's a Halloween parade or something and the little boy waves bye. Then it's supper time. Okay?"

Chip looked up innocently at Bennie, his head tilted slightly, awaiting her response. She turned to me. "Did you guys make all this up?"

Patiently, Chip clarified, "No, Mom. We really saw it on television. It was just a little boy dressed up in a ghost outfit 'cause he wanted to be just like his dad. Only his daddy wasn't playing. He was really scared and pretending he wasn't. That's all."

Out of the mouth of babes.

IMPROVING YOUR PARENTING ART

1. Develop a positive attitude toward life and specifically your child. Examine what you are critical about in regard to your child. Can you separate the behavior from the behaver and verbalize these differences with your child?

2. Respect your child as a human being. For example, consider her needs for privacy, to be listened to, and to have opinions differing from yours.

3. Develop a sensitivity to his feelings. Be willing to listen to him without being distracted by any other activity.

4. Schedule time to spend with your child on a regular basis. Allow the child to decide how the time will be spent and honor her choices.

5. Practice verbalizing your love for your child. Remember, it is impossible to truly love another person until you truly love yourself.

6. Set up opportunities for your child to develop meaningful relationships with other significant adults: a relative, pastor, neighbor, or friend. Note and discuss with your child whom he admires.

7. Be clear and consistent in your communications with your child. Share your honest feelings, so that your verbal and nonverbal responses match.

8. Encourage your child to express her own feelings. Then do not contradict, deny, or scold. Praise the child for her willingness to trust you.

9. Reward verbally any attempts made by your child to overcome an obstacle, try a new adventure, or overcome a fear. Give continuing support for all similar efforts.

PARENTING EXERCISES

Study the following lists. Work toward increasing your use of words and phrases in the first list and toward decreasing your use of those in the second list.

Words and Phrases that Motivate

Challenge	You can do it
Opportunity	Yes, you can
Beautiful	Go for it
Terrific	It's possible
Perfect	Thank you
Super	That's very good
I'm pleased	I appreciate your
I agree	good work
You are improving	You can do anything
Good thinking	I believe in you
Excellent idea	Keep up the good work

Words and Phrases that Discourage

Problem	Be careful
However	Better watch out
Never	That's impossible
It's your fault	Something bad
You make me . . .	might happen
You can't do that	What's the problem
You might get hurt	I demand
That's bad	

Just as the twig is bent, the tree's inclined.
—*Alexander Pope*

Do to others as you would have them do to you.
—*Luke 6:31*

10

Cherish Your Child's Individuality

I HAD BEEN invited to speak at a convention in Charlotte, North Carolina, which I consider my home town. The sponsors flew Bennie and me to Charlotte in a small corporate plane. It was the first time we had flown in such a plush aircraft. We were met at the airport by a limousine driver who was to take us downtown to the meeting. Nestled in the backseat, we reminisced about the early days of our marriage when we lived in the Charlotte area.

"Look." Bennie pointed. "We used to eat at that restaurant. Remember?"

"Yeah." I nodded. "Good ribs, huh?"

"Uh-huh," she agreed. "But you know what I remember about it? I remember how different it was back then. Remember what it was like? You wouldn't ever go in there if there were more than four or five cars out front. Do you remember?"

I thought for a moment. "Yeah," I sighed. "I remember."

"It seems like another lifetime." Bennie sighed. "I remem-

ber when we'd be out somewhere talking and if anybody else stopped by you'd get up and leave. You really were uncomfortable around others back then."

"Yes," I agreed. "I was. It seems like a long time ago. Almost like I was a different person."

"Do you remember what it was like after Vietnam? You wouldn't laugh or cry, but when you felt any emotions your chin would quiver. Remember?"

My mind raced to the terrariumlike jungles of Vietnam. "Yes, I remember it all," I said, nodding.

"You would never have spoken to a group back then. You would hardly talk to anyone but your mother and me."

"I guess I figured nobody else would understand."

"You used to sort of check out," Bennie continued. "It was like you'd detach and withdraw. I never knew how to help you back then. It scared me to death."

"You helped me fine," I assured her. "You just hung in there and stood by. That was all I needed. You anchored me to reality."

"You haven't had a nightmare in years," she said cautiously. "I can remember when I'd wake up and you'd be shaking and soaking wet from sweat. Then you'd scream. I was always so frightened."

"So was I. It's a long way, isn't it?"

"It sure is." She smiled. "And now here you are. They're expecting about twelve hundred people at the conference. I'm really proud of you. You've come a long way in fifteen years."

"Well, fifteen years is a long time." But as I thought about it, I realized it seemed like yesterday.

APPRECIATE UNIQUENESS

Just like a fingerprint, each child's personality is unique. At birth, even identical twins have totally different personalities. One must approach a child as the individual he or she is.

The alternative is a dangerous one indeed. In one case it almost fractured an entire family.

Over the past months I had grown very close to this family. It had taken eleven family therapy sessions for us to reach this peak moment.

George sat on the couch, vigorously attacking his chewing gum. His large arms filled the short sleeves of his shirt as he leaned nervously on his knees. George still had the look of a boyish athlete, though by now he was in his late thirties. His wife, Martha, sat beside him. Her hands were clasped together on her lap, and she looked up at her husband almost protectively. On the other side of Martha sat their sixteen-year-old daughter, Amy. She alternately looked at me and her father as if to measure our response.

And then there was Tommy. He was a small wisp of a fourteen-year-old. Everything about Tommy was skinny. You could see some resemblance between Tommy and his father in their faces, but otherwise Tommy appeared to be the exact opposite of his father. In his small hand, Tommy held a sheet of papers at which he gazed.

"Tommy, why don't you read your list," I urged. We had been in the session for a few minutes, and I had greeted each family member.

The silence was broken only by George's loud gum chewing. Tommy coughed to clear his throat.

"Now?" Tommy asked uncertainly.

I nodded. Tommy looked at his list and coughed again.

"I resent that when I was a little you used to quit passing the football with me if I threw a bad one. I resent the time you left me outside and went in the house because I threw the ball over your head. I resent the fact that you never told me I was doing a good job."

As Tommy continued to read his list of resentments, I silently recalled how the family had come to this point. George had never gotten beyond his image as a college football player. Although now he was a salesman, he still looked like a jock.

His hair was cut short, and he walked with a self-confident swagger. He volunteered as an assistant football coach for a local high school, entered racketball tournaments, and jogged five miles per day regardless of the weather.

When Tommy was a toddler, George had unrealistic expectations of him. The demands were so great that Tommy could never gain George's approval. Out of frustration Tommy slowly gave up. Eventually he made an unconscious choice to be as different from his father as possible. Without knowing it, Tommy was angry and wanted to get even. He rejected his father's values as one way of expressing his anger. Now we were trying to deal with the anger in a more constructive, though also more threatening, way. Much pain and struggling had preceded this moment.

Tommy continued to read.

"I resent that I could not live up to your standards. But most of all I resent that you never have seemed to love me. All I ever wanted from you was to be loved. That's the reason I'm so angry."

Tommy stopped reading but continued staring at his paper. Nobody broke the silence. George even quit chewing his gum. This family had been fractured by the emotional distance between father and son. At one point the two had gone seven months without as much as speaking to each other. But their mutual silence was aggressive. Instead of playing football as his dad wanted, Tommy took piano lessons. Rather than develop an interest in competitive pursuits, Tommy joined the drama club. And instead of jogging with his father, Tommy cross-stitched with his mother. Just as George had rejected Tommy, Tommy had rejected George. Their impasse was broken when Martha insisted the family enter counseling.

I looked at George. His gaze was fixed in front of him. Amy and Martha both cried softly. The charged atmosphere became almost reverent. I started to speak several times, but stopped short. I waited instead.

"You know," George's voice cracked. "You know, Tommy.

You're different from me in some ways and similar to me in others. All these things I've been doing—they're all things my dad did to me. I was never good enough for him. He never gave me a pat on the back. Not once did he ever say he was proud of me. I kept on trying. Maybe if I make All-Conference, All-State, All-American, but it was never enough. He never gave me anything. And I remember thinking, I'll never do that to my kid. But you know what? You're different. I'd never have the guts to face up to my father and tell him how I felt. You're more of a man than I'll ever be, Tommy. I've underestimated you. Forgive me. I love you so much."

Tommy dropped his papers and ran into his father's huge embrace. They began sobbing together. Over the next several months, many changes started. Tommy entered a weight lifting program at his high school. He gained over twenty pounds of muscle within two years. His physical appearance and mannerisms changed dramatically. To George's delight, Tommy was starting varsity quarterback on the football team during his senior year of high school. George claimed it really didn't matter. There was no pressure on Tommy to achieve in sports now. But the pride and approval was obvious. The individual respect for each other's uniquenesses within the family overcame thirteen years of distance.

CHERISH YOUR CHILD

I think there are ten questions to determine if one is cherishing a child individually. They are based on both research and professional experience. However, unlike most other comments I have made in this book, these are based more on my professional opinion than on scientific studies. It's impossible to make any claim to their empirical validity. I can say, though, that hundreds of parents have found them extremely helpful.

1. *Do I recognize each child as being different and unique*

from others? Anyone who has contact with more than one child from the same family will agree. Personalities are as different as fingerprints. No two are identical. In fact, even twins can have radically different personalities. This reality makes comparisons counterproductive and occasionally even destructive.

Even with the awareness that each child is different, some parents make the mistake of comparing them aloud. Others do not, but have unspoken expectations that one child should resemble another in some behavioral way. As discussed in an earlier chapter, it's doubtful these expectations can be disguised or concealed. At some level, they will be communicated to your children. And in no way can this be positive, even if the comparison is a favorable one. The mere act of comparison is destructive.

2. *Can I be perceived by my child as consistent and reliable?* My children, though young, are people nonetheless. Keeping this in mind helps me be honest with them. But more importantly, it helps my children. If my behavior toward them is consistent, it will help them feel more certain in their approach to me. A child who is put in the position of constantly second-guessing parents will have difficulty forming relationships as an adult.

If I am reliable with my children, my thoughts, feelings, behavior, and words will be consistent. I refuse to be unpredictable to my children. In this way I become dependable and worthy of their trust.

An example of this phenomenon illustrates the power and influence of modeling. I worked with Russell in counseling for several months. He was an extremely successful physician and businessman, but extremely unsuccessful in his interpersonal relationships. In fact, after only a few sessions it became evident that Russell was totally fearful of intimacy. As long as a relationship was superficial, he had no difficulty with it. But once anyone began getting close, he would do something to achieve distance. If the person was a family member, Russell would start an argument. If the person was a business associate, Russell would either start an argument or fire him or her! In fact, the employee turnover rate in his medical practice was phenomenal. Yet, on a superficial or professional level, Russell functioned extremely well.

Although Russell was from a family of six siblings, he had not had any contact with them in many years. His parental relationships were strained to the point of a near emotional cutoff. His business partners, who had grown weary of Russell's tantrumlike outbursts, shunned him personally. His wife and children had learned to balance the family functions while keeping Russell at a safe distance.

It was obvious to me from the beginning of our discussions that Russell's problem had started during childhood and was now chronic in nature. Russell disclosed that both parents were alcoholics. During his childhood, Russell never knew what to expect from them. At one moment they were loving and responsive to his needs. The next, they could be drunk and abusive. As a result of these early learning experiences, Russell apparently made several assumptions.

One of these assumptions was that people who get close to you will end up hurting you. Therefore, to avoid pain, avoid closeness. Another decision Russell made was to not trust people. After all, he reasoned, if you can't trust your own parents, who can you trust? It was a good question to ask, but nearly impossible to answer. Apparently, at some deep level, Russell made another decision. He decided to focus on busyness as a way to avoid emotions. Emotions were confusing, intimidating, and hurtful. Deep relationships represented pain. Russell figured he had experienced enough of that during childhood. Unfortunately, by cutting off his emotions, he had also cut off love.

He almost figured it out. But he got scared. I got too close and he cut me off, too.

3. *Am I responding to my child as she is at a given moment?* Responding to the reality in front of you is often

difficult to do. It means ignoring your fears, resentments, and egocentric needs and focusing exclusively on your child *as she is*. Staying in the here and now is a difficult challenge. To some people it's almost impossible. We have all spent time around someone who seemed to enjoy living in the past. That in itself can be very destructive. But if you judge others by their past mistakes, the level of pain caused can even be doubled. To avoid this, remain in the moment and respond to your child as she is, not as she has been in the past or may be in the future.

It's important to realize that children are affected by their perceptions and not necessarily by reality. In fact, reality often is irrelevant to a child. As an example, if they ask your permission to do something and you say no, suddenly they may accuse you of not loving them. Probably every parent of a teenager has experienced this to one degree or another, and it can be wearisome. It is easy to allow such experiences as these to build up and actually become resentments over time. If resentments, grievances, or memories from past problems are allowed to accumulate, you can begin to see your child through clouded glasses of the past rather than as they are.

4. *Can I be strong enough to respect my child's separateness from me and love her anyway?* In a recent counseling session, Sheila, an energetic eighteen-year-old high-school senior disclosed to her mother a recent sexual involvement. Her mother, Reba, exploded. In an argument that took place after our session, Reba called her daughter a slut, among other things.

"How can you say you love your daddy and me when you do something like that?" she demanded.

"Mother," Sheila groaned. "That had nothing to do with you. It was Jeff and me. It was a mistake, certainly. But you act like I did it directly to you. It had nothing to do with you. It was my body, not yours!"

"I didn't say you did it directly to me," Reba defended.

"But if you loved your parents, you wouldn't do something like that. That's all."

"I'm eighteen!" Sheila shouted. "And I *am* different than you, you know?"

Through a great deal of effort and compromise, Reba and Sheila were able to heal their wounds. And Sheila later made a decision to cease her sexual involvement. Yet, the damage already caused did have a permanent effect. Reba didn't seem to realize that Sheila was a separate individual and would make separate and not always parentally approved decisions. There are ways to disagree with your adult children. But Reba's method was probably not the most helpful in either content or process. She acted as if Sheila's behavior was a direct extension of hers. As a result, over the following few weeks, Reba's love was perceived as withdrawn.

"It's almost like she loves me as long as I have my virginity." Sheila shrugged her shoulders. "Or, like I love you as long as you do exactly what I want you to do. What kind of love is that, John? And whose body is this anyway? Is it mine or my mother's? I know what I did was a mistake, but this just isn't right."

Cherishing your child means you allow them to be separate and respect their separateness. This doesn't mean you will approve of everything they do. But it does mean you will love and respect them regardless of their separateness. It's a difficult thing to do. Yet, it's paramount for your child's emotional development.

5. *Am I willing to attempt to understand my child's world from the inside out?* I once read that you'll never truly understand another person. That sentiment is probably accurate. Completely understanding another is virtually impossible. However, it is important to make an attempt to see the world as your child sees it.

This process involves a nonevaluative approach to comprehending what your child sees, hears, thinks, and feels. It is not feeling sorry for your children. It is feeling along with them. To accomplish this you have to lose a great deal of yourself and almost climb inside your child's emotional world. It requires incredible intensity, focused attention on the child, and unfathomable energy. But your child will feel cherished, which makes it worth the effort.

6. *Am I secure enough in my own beliefs that I can refrain from any tendency to judge or criticize?* I have been involved in some aspect of the counseling profession continually since 1974. During that period I have witnessed or been told of hundreds of times when family members have been unmercifully critical toward each other. Often, these criticisms are directed from parents toward a child. Sometimes toward a spouse. Whatever the case, I have made several assumptions concerning such criticism.

First, I believe it is based on a fear that the other person's ideas or behavior in some way threatens my own security. Several years ago my mother complained to me about the child of one of her friends. "Oh, Mom," I teased. "He's just being a teenager. I did the same kind of stuff myself when I was that age."

"No, you didn't," she insisted. "I never had that kind of trouble with you."

"Mom," I laughed. "How about the time—" And I continued to remind her of several occasions when I had done things similar to her friend's teenager.

"Hush, Son," she interrupted. "I don't want to remember!" Actually, Mom was afraid I was right. And she didn't want to hear anymore! We all often engage in similar logic. If someone is going to disrupt the way we think, it may be less painful to simply ignore him. If we are hostile or critical of his ideas maybe he will keep them to himself!

Another assumption is more personal. For years I was critical of my wife. She didn't think right or talk right. After it was almost too late, I realized that I was demanding that she think and act like me! This wasn't a conscious awareness at first, but it had certainly affected my behavior. Since that time,

I have found this to be true among many family members. Often, when we are critical or demanding of another person, we're really telling them to be more like me. Your need to judge them originates from a fear of what they will be like if they're different from you. Because if they are different from you, their behavior is more unpredictable.

The final assumption has to do with the moral implication. We often criticize what we don't understand and then label it as wrong or bad. In reality it may only be different, but out of fear, we define it as wrong. Some of the dangerous people in the universe mean well. They truly want to help people, but their attitude is one that says "if you don't believe just like I do, you're immoral." I have worked in several different settings with people who project this attitude. They all have the best of intentions, but they cause more pain and suffering than one could ever imagine. And each of these people I have gotten to know share one deep emotion in common. They are all extremely insecure.

7. *Can I accept my child as in the constant process of change?* It's a paradox that we change while remaining the same. The hand that wrote this book is the same one that scrawled out the ABCs as a first grader years ago. At the same time, it's much different in size, dexterity, and appearance. It's the same. But it's different! The same paradox is true with all children. They are the same from day to day. But at the same time, they're very different. The one constant you can depend on is change!

Change occurs at varying times and paces. During the first year of life, changes occur with lightning speed. Then it slows for a few years. Then again in adolescence, the speed of change is so rapid that it's almost impossible to keep up. Neither the adolescent nor the parents know what to expect. Some parents assume change to be a negative concept. Since it is a natural process, this attitude can be very destructive to a child. Referring back to the chapter on expectations, you'll see that such beliefs are always communicated to your child and will inevitably affect his behavior. It's best for your child and you as a parent to accept growth as normal and desirable. Develop an attitude of excitement about your child's changes and look forward to them. This will be communicated to your child and will ease the transition process.

8. *Am I willing to compromise some of my own egocentric needs to be a facilitator of my child's growth?* I have been faced in dozens of counseling sessions with what happens to children when their parents continually put their own needs first. This is most often done, unfortunately, by fathers. You can place hundreds of things in a position of greater importance than your children. And your priorities will be communicated in some way to your children. These priorities can be Dad's job, sports, or even church. Even in the name of God, ignoring your child can have devastating results.

Certainly, there are times when we all need one more hour on the job, or when we'd like to play nine more holes of golf. But the needs of your child are great. And to truly cherish your child means placing him in a position of far greater importance than anything else.

To truly cherish your children requires compromise. Parenting at its best is an unselfish act of love. It's a gift of spontaneous generosity over the years, and requires continual sacrifice. That is actually the goal parents can strive toward as we continually seek to improve our talents as parental artists. Needless to say, the striving demands much blood, sweat, and tears.

Much has been said about parents who "remain married for the children." Some professionals say it's ridiculous. Others say the child's needs would be served better if the parents would go ahead and separate. There is some research to support both sides of the issue. By my account, the overwhelming evidence is clear. It indicates, although there are exceptions, it's better for a child to have both parents at home; almost regardless of the circumstances. I have worked with many families in which parents have sacrificed their own desires and remained married for the sake of the children.

I worked with one couple who got divorced and bought a duplex. Dad lived on one side. Mother lived on the other. The children lived on both sides and had constant access to both parents. Mom and Dad were able to be civil to each other, and the children benefited tremendously. This arrangement continued until both children left home to enter college. The parents then parted as friends and went their separate ways. It was one of the most mature and unselfish acts of love in which I have ever been involved.

9. *Am I willing to accept my child as imperfect?* It seems obvious, yet we so easily forget. We are all imperfect. Awhile ago I received a phone call from a friend who apologized for something that had occurred some time earlier. I had been deeply hurt by what this person had done, and had suffered both emotionally and financially as a result. After his apology, I paused for a moment.

"I guess you're just like me," I finally said. "And I expect and accept imperfection from you. I hope you can accept it from me. Because I'm sure I'll make mistakes in the future."

Your child is going to make mistakes. That's a big part of being human. It means she's normal. I don't see it as helpful or healthy to be critical of your child for being human. In fact, I model imperfection for my children. The yoke of perfection is incredibly cumbersome and destructive for a child to bear. It is constantly accompanied by guilt and shame. This can lead to a position of low self worth and eventually self-destructiveness.

Cherishing your child means accepting her as she is— imperfect and human.

10. *Can I love my child, regardless of what he does, and project a sense of unconditional positive regard?* The early chapters of this book elaborate on the quality of unconditional acceptance. The importance and value of this for your children cannot be underestimated. It would be redundant to cover all the material again. Nevertheless, any comments on cherishing

your children would be woefully incomplete without mention of this essential ingredient to successful parenting.

STREET SMARTS

Parents can answer all these questions appropriately and still have children who have problems. This happens for two reasons. First, many factors influence your children other than you. Second, your children have freedom of choice. I have worked with hundreds of parents who think they failed because their children made bad choices. Personally, I think it's normal for all of us to make bad choices. So I feel no guilt when my children err.

If there is one place where well-intentioned parents often fail, it's in not teaching their children what I call street smarts. To me, part of cherishing your children includes teaching them this quality. Those who possess it have a distinct advantage in everyday life. My youngest son, Chip, seems to come by this naturally. I once gave him a cookie in bed, which is directly against one of his mom's rules. Chip gladly took it, nevertheless, and attacked it in a fashion that would have pleased the "cookie monster" himself!

Later he got up and came in the den where Bennie and I were talking.

"Son," Bennie spoke to him for the second time that evening. "You have got to go to bed right now."

"Daddy gave me a cookie again," Chip tattled.

Bennie immediately turned toward me. "Why did you do that?" she asked. "You know they're not supposed to eat in bed!"

Taking a cue from Chip, I immediately changed the subject. "Do you realize what just happened?" I looked at her.

"What?" She looked at me sternly.

"He just split us," I laughed. "He changed the subject so

you would talk to me. Now he will stay up while we talk about cookies!"

She immediately turned toward Chip. "No matter what your daddy did, you still have to go to bed, Son." Then she escorted Chip to his bed. Later I was confronted by her for bootlegging illegal cookies. My splitting didn't work. Bennie is street smart too.

Street smarts is something that can and should be taught. One place to start is in the area of communication dynamics. You can teach your child that the way communication takes place is as important as what's being said. One family illustrated this point quite well.

Doug was an attorney for a local city government. Stephanie, his wife, worked as a nurse part-time and spent more than full time keeping up with their spunky, red-haired, ten-year-old named Sonia. On one occasion we were all together when Doug was scolding Sonia for getting in trouble at school.

"You have got to put a stop to this," he demanded. "I'm tired of these notes coming home. Just quit playing with those kids if you're going to stay in trouble all the time."

"Now, Daddy." She faced him squarely and placed her hands on her hips. "It's not my fault. They chase me. All I do is run. Those dumb boys should get in trouble, not me. But I'm the one who gets caught all the time."

"That's because you're part of the conspiracy," he said firmly. "Collusion in a crime makes you guilty of the crime."

"Wait a minute, Doug," I butted in. "Let's think about this. What would happen, Sonia, if you didn't run."

"Huh, what do you mean?"

"Say the guy comes to chase you and you just stare at him or something. Tell him you don't want to play chase and then walk away. What would happen?"

She looked at the ceiling. "I don't know. They couldn't chase me if I didn't run."

"Right," I agreed. "It takes two people to play chase. One person has to start, and the other has to run away. If both people don't cooperate, there is no game. You can't make the boys not chase you. But you can refuse to play the game.''

She did refuse, the very next day. Doug called me on the phone and gave me the news. "She said that she looked the guy in the eye and told him chase was a stupid game and it was for kids. That she was too old and didn't want to play silly games. Then apparently she turned and left. No game.''

"Great!" I laughed. "Looks like we've created a mankiller, huh?''

The ability to assert yourself and refuse to play games is part of being street smart. Teaching Sonia to say no to chase will help her say no to a lot of other games in her future. She will face lots of people in life who will try to lure her into trouble. But teaching her street smarts at this early age will help her survive those attempts.

We live in a society where the family has assumed a subordinate position to technology and industry. The competition for a family's attention is fierce. The only resolution is for the corporate community to value and recognize the importance of family structure in social life. This has already begun to occur in some companies. But the number is still far too few. Awareness of the importance of family is long overdue and welcomed by both parents and children.

I was guest at a radio talk show in Dallas, Texas, when I heard a cheery Southern twang come through the earphones. "Is this Dr. Baucom?" a female voice sang.

"Yes, ma'am," I responded. "Thank you for calling.''

"Well, doctor, I have a question to ask you. My husband has just been promoted to the vice-presidency of his company and—''

"Congratulations!" I interrupted. "Tell your husband I said congratulations.''

"Well, thank you!" Her voice seemed to smile. "You're very sweet. Well, anyway, my husband got promoted, but we're going to have to move to Miami in three weeks. And I was wondering. Do you think I should tell my seventeen-year-old daughter or surprise her? What do you think?"

I sat in stunned silence, waiting for the punch line, or the gag. "You're serious, aren't you?"

"Hmm?" she seemed startled. "Oh, of course I'm serious. Why do you ask?"

"Let me make sure I understand this. Your husband just got promoted, and you're going to move to Miami in three weeks. You have a seventeen-year-old daughter who doesn't know anything at all about this. Is that right, ma'am?"

"Uh-huh," she confessed. "I didn't want to worry her or anything. So I haven't told her. I don't think she's going to be too excited about moving. She's a senior cheerleader next year and everything. So we're just not sure what to do. But the company calls and we have to answer."

One of the good things about this phone call was it occurred on a radio talk show rather than on TV. I must have had a look of horror on my face. The host kept staring at me. Finally, I was able to respond.

"Ma'am," I pronounced each word very slowly and clearly. "This is very important, and I want you to understand exactly how I feel. Unless there is some very convincing reason why your husband insists you move to Miami, I would suggest you consider staying in Dallas. Teenagers have committed suicide because of stuff like this. If I were you, I would strongly consider staying in Dallas with your daughter one more year. After she graduates and is in college, then you can join your husband in Miami. Otherwise, I think you might be making a very big mistake for your daughter and the entire family."

We continued to talk for a few more minutes. Several days after I had returned home, I had a message to return a call to Dallas. The same syrupy voice sang out hello.

"Well, I just wanted to tell you what we decided to do." She informed me that the entire family had made a decision. She and her daughter would remain in Dallas until her daughter graduated. They would visit her husband in Miami several times during the school year. After her daughter completed the school year they both would go to Miami for the summer. Sometime later, the daughter would decide what her plans would be for the future.

"I'm glad I talked to you," the caller confessed. "Joanie told me she never would have gone, whether it meant running away or whatever. She really seemed to appreciate my willingness to stay here one more year. Thank you."

Bennie's comments had sent me into my own world. I turned and looked out the car window and saw the entrance to a local radio station. I recalled a visit to the same station thirty years earlier with my father. And once again I reflected on his death.

I wondered how my life would have changed if he had not died. I probably wouldn't have played football, I figured. We would have moved too often. I learned to struggle against the odds by playing football. Also, I would never have met the Gilmers, nor Jim Murray, nor Joe McLeod. All of these people had been instrumental in my spiritual development. And if it weren't for all of them I would probably have had no religious faith whatever. I even lived with Barret and Dudley Gilmer for quite some time. That would not have happened without the death of my father.

My eyes followed the reflection of our car speeding across the darkly tinted windows of an office building. My thoughts soared to the steam bath jungles of Vietnam. I recalled the names of my close friends, some of whom I had watched die. Where are the survivors now, I wondered. I saw the childlike faces of the Mountangaard family with whom Andor and I had lived.

Then I smiled as I recalled one of the last conversations Andor and I ever had. During a weekend in Da Nang, I had wanted to get a tattoo. "You no need tattoo, Yonathan," he scolded in his Hungarian-accented English. "I tell you what,

Son, every time you hear helicopter for rest of life, you remember Vietnam. You remember Andor. No matter how old, you remember. Helicopter be your tattoo." His comments have proved prophetic.

A week later he was dead, and shortly thereafter I lay in a hospital bed in Germany. That was where I met Bennie. If we had not been at that place in that time, we would have never met. My eyes began to swell with tears. I turned to face her.

"I'm sorry," she apologized. "I talk too much. I had no right—"

"No—no." I reached out and touched her hand. "It's not that at all. I was just sitting here thinking. Things are beginning to come together. Like a big jigsaw puzzle. The pieces are beginning to make sense."

I turned and looked out the window again as we passed by several familiar landmarks. If I had not played football, I would never have learned to struggle. If it hadn't been for the influence of three men, I would never have developed any spiritual depth. Without the ability to struggle against the odds, I would never have received my assignment as an advisor in Vietnam. Without the spiritual depth, I never would have survived Vietnam.

If I had not received the assignment as an advisor, I would never have met Andor. If I had not met Andor, I would not have gotten wounded when I did. If I had not gotten wounded, I would never have ended up as a patient in a German hospital. If I had not been in that hospital, I would never have met Bennie.

If I had never met Bennie, I would never have gotten out of the military service and returned to the college I did. Then I would not have gone to the counselor I went to. He was primarily responsible for me being a counselor today. If I had not been a counselor, I would never have written a book. And if I had not written a book, I would not have received the invitation to speak at the conference.

It's one big cycle. Bonding and breaking free. I bonded

with my family in early childhood and with others after my father's death. Then later, I broke free, not only from those early dependencies, but from my fears and from the past. It was all important. Every link was necessary. Good can come from tragedies. And with God's and man's cherishing and cooperative help, people can overcome obstacles in today's world.

IMPROVING YOUR PARENTING ART

Record the positive ways in which you see your child as different from yourself. The next time you and your child disagree, tape record the argument. When you have cooled down, listen to it and analyze your words and attitudes. Did you allow the child to be different from you? Did you express unconditional acceptance of the child apart from his behavior?

PARENTING EXERCISES

The following themes recur in all families. How we deal with them has much to do with the degree of success we experience as members of a unique family. Consider these as possible discussion topics for family meetings. Also, consider the possibility of including grandparents for appropriate topics.

1. We learn child-rearing practices, both good and bad, from our parents.

2. A family has a collective personality and is only as strong as its weakest link. If one family member hurts, all members share the hurt.

3. We each are mapping our own courses. We all make our own choices. Even the claim that we don't have a choice is a choice we make. Every obstacle can be overcome as we proceed toward achieving our maximum potential.

4. Children are not miniature adults. Their feelings are not miniature feelings; hurts are not miniature hurts; experiences not miniature experiences. All children are completely human in every aspect of their lives.

EPILOGUE

Isabelle, the child mentioned early in this book who was locked in a closet with her deaf and mute mother, had every reason in the world to give up. She had every right to be miserable. No one expected her to do anything but die. Yet today she is reportedly a healthy and beautiful grandmother.

My young friend Andy, left to die in a filthy trash dumpster, could have given up on many occasions. But the sting of multiple rejections and the emotional sterility of institutional life could not empty him. Today he is in graduate school and works as a teaching assistant at a university.

Both of these people had family members who made mistakes. Yet each overcame the tremendous obstacles of early childhood problems and now has a full and healthy life. There is no magic formula that explains why these people flourished and why others who suffered far less difficulty crumbled.

As a parent, I have the responsibility to do whatever I can to prepare each of my children for a healthy life. I have an obligation to learn what I can about parenting and to do the best I can to raise my children in a healthy way. But at some vague point in time, the responsibility shifts to the child. My children cannot do my job as a parent, and I cannot do theirs as separate and unique individuals.

If I could somehow do everything right as a parent, my children could still make bad decisions as adults. On the other hand, if I were to make every possible parenting mistake, my children might still make good decisions as adults. Objective evidence demonstrates, however, that my children are much more likely to make good decisions as adults if I follow well-researched principles in preparing them for life.

That's why I wrote this book. I intend to do my job as a father. And I will do my best to prepare them for the joyful occasion when they assume responsibility. If they make some bad choices along the way, I will welcome them to the human race and love them anyway.

Daddy makes mistakes, too.

BIBLIOGRAPHY

Baldwin, *et al.* "Patterns of Parenting Behavior." *Psychological Monographs*, LVIII (1945), 1–75.

Baumrind, Diana. "The Development of Instrumental Competence Through Socialization." *Vol. VII of Minnesota Symposium on Child Psychology*. Edited by Ann D. Peck. 9 vols. Minneapolis: University of Minnesota Press, 1973.

Baumrind, D. "The Development of Instrumental Competence Through Socialization." Vol. VII of *Minnesota Symposium on Child Psychology*. Edited by Ann D. Peck. 9 vols. Minneapolis: The University of Minnesota Press, 1973.

Berne, Eric. *What Do You Say After You Say Hello*. New York: Grove Press, 1972.

Bowlby, John. *Child Care and the Growth of Love*. Baltimore: Penguin, 1953.

Bowling, John. *Attachment and Loss*. New York: Basic Books, 1969.

Coopersmith, Stanley. *The Antecedents of Self-Esteem*. San Francisco: W. H. Freeman, 1967.

Cozby, Paul. "Self Disclosure: A Literature Review." *Psychological Bulletin*, LXXIX (1973), 73–91.

Davis, Kingsley. "Final Note on a Case of Extreme Isolation." *The American Journal of Sociology*, (March, 1947), 432–37.

Dennis, W. *Children of the Creche*. New York: Appleton-Century-Crofts, 1973.

Dittes, J. E. "Galvanic Skin Response As a Measure of Patients' Reaction to Therapist." *Journal of Abnormal and Social Psychology*, LV (1957), 295–303.

Erikson, Erick. *Children and Society.* New York: W. W. Norton & Co., 1963.

Erikson, E. H. *Childhood and Society.* New York: W. W. Norton & Co., 1963.

Fredricks, A. H. *Labeling of Students by Prospective Teachers.* Chicago: American Educational Research Association, 1974.

Furman, Erma. "The Innermost Child." *Psychoanalytic Survey of the Child,* XXXVII (1982), 15−28.

Gardner, L. "Deprivation Dwarfism." *Scientific American,* CCXXVII (July, 1972), 76−82.

Gelles, Richard; Straus, Murray; and Steinmetz, Suzanne. *Violence in the American Family.* Garden City, N.J.: Doubleday, Anchor Press, 1978.

Gibson, Janice and Wurst, Karen. "Delinquency: A Family Issue." *International Journal of Psychology,* XIX (January, 1984), 241−44.

Gill, D. G. *Violence Against Children.* Cambridge, Mass.: Harvard University Press, 1970.

Ginott, Haim G. *Between Parent and Child.* New York: Avon, 1969.

Ginott, H. G. *Between Parent and Teenager.* New York: Avon, 1971.

Goldfarb, William. "Psychological Privation in Infancy and Subsequent Adjustment." *American Journal of Orthopsychiatry,* XV (1945), 247−53.

Good, T. L.; Biddle, B. J.; and Brophy, J. E. *Teachers Make a Difference.* New York: Holt, Rinehart & Winston, 1975.

Gordon, Thomas. *P.E.T. Parent Effectiveness Training.* New York: New American Library, 1975.

Greiger, Tonya; Kaufman, James; and Greiger, Russell. "Effects of Peer Reporting or Cooperative Play and Aggression of Kindergarten Children." *Journal of School Psychology,* XIV (1977), 307−13.

Hall, Edward T. *The Silent Language.* New York: Doubleday & Co., 1959.

Harlow, H. F. and Harlow, M. K. "The Young Monkeys." *Psychology Today,* (September, 1967), 41−47.

Harlow, H. F., *et al.* "Total Social Isolation in Monkeys." Vol. LIV of *Proceedings of the National Academy of Sciences.* 201 vols. New York: Scientific Press, 1965.

Heatherington, E. M. "Effects of Paternal Absence on Sextyped Behaviors in Black and White Pre-adolescent Males." *Journal of Personality and Social Psychology*, (1966), 4, 87–91.

Holly, Peggy. "Teresa Trower Elementary School Guidance and Counseling." *Journal of Social Issues*, XIX (December, 1984), 147–51.

Insel, P. and Jacobson, L. *What Do You Expect? An Inquiry into Self-Fulfilling Prophecies*. Menlo Park, Calif.: Cummings, 1975.

Jourard, Sidney. *The Transparent Self*. Revised. New York: Van Nostrand Reinhold, 1971.

Keeson. W. *The Child*. New York: John Wiley & Sons, 1965.

Klaus, M. H. and Kemmel, J. H. *Maternal-Infant Bonding*. St. Louis: C. V. Mosby Co., 1976.

Konerski, Edward; Crowell, Charles; and Duggan, Leo. "The Use of Response Deprivation to Increase the Academic Performance of EMR Students." *Applied Research on Mental Retardation*, VI (1985), 15–31.

Lee, G. R. *Family Structure and Interaction: A Comparative Analysis*. Philadelphia: J. B. Lippincott Co., 1977.

Lewis, Michael, *et al*. *Child Influences on Marital and Family Interaction: A Life-span Perspective*. New York: Academic Press, 1978.

Longern, R., *et al*. "Industrialized Family Mobility and Its Impact on Society." *Bulletin of the American Academy of Psychiatry and the Law*, XI (1983), 331–41.

Lorenz, K. Z. "Imprinting." *Instinct*. Edited by R. C. Birney and R. C. Teevan. London: Van Nostrand Reinhold Co., 1961.

Maccoby, Eleanor and Feldman, Shirley. *Mother Attachment and Stranger Reactions in the Third Year of Life*. Vol. XXXVII of *Monographs of the Society for Research in Child Development*. 37 vols. Stanford, Calif.: Stanford University Press, 1972.

Martin, Lawrence. "Self-Image and Development." *New York Times*, (March 20, 1977), 5–6.

Maslow, Abraham H. *Toward a Psychology of Being*. 2nd ed. New York: Van Nostrand Reinhold Co., 1968.

Maslow, A. H. *Toward a Psychology of Being*. Princeton, N.J.: Van Nostrand Reinhold Co., 1968.